In the Moments of God
My Journey of Faith and Transplantation

By Kenneth Parkes

Self published in 2012 by Kenneth Parkes

Copyright © Kenneth Parkes 2012

ISBN 978-1-291-05157-5

First Edition 2012
Printed and bound by www.Lulu.com

Front cover photograph: Medjugorje Sunset © Kenneth Parkes

In the Moments of God
My Journey of Faith and Transplantation

Introduction

My name is Kenneth Parkes; I was born on the 27th of June 1975, in Dublin, Ireland. Known to everyone as Ken, I am the middle child of Anne and David. Lorna, my sister is two years older and Gary, my brother is six years younger than me. I live in Tallaght, a suburb of Dublin. I was bought up a Catholic, but it was not such a part of our daily lives. We went to Mass on Sundays and said a short prayer before bedtime.

I was a sickly infant and at ten months old I was diagnosed as having Cystic Fibrosis. My Parents had never heard of Cystic Fibrosis before, so it was a shock for them both. Fortunately, after an unhealthy first ten months my health improved and I led a reasonably healthy life. I began going to school at four years of age and finished school just before my 17th birthday. I was rarely in hospital and only had four admissions in twenty-three years. However in January 1999 my health worsened and I eventually needed a double lung transplant.

My book tells of this journey and how I turned away from God and subsequently how I got to know Him again in a place called Medjugorje, a small village in Bosnia Herzegovina. I started writing this book when I was sick, not knowing the outcome. It's a very honest account of my journey and I hope you enjoy reading my story as much as I have enjoyed writing it. I pray it helps you on your own journey. I was always hoping for that happy ending. I came to realise during this journey that there would, and could only be a happy ending because knowing God's Love for me is enough.

One evening in September 2000 Fr. Svetozar kraljevic a priest from Medjugorje, 'Fr. Svet' as he is known to the many pilgrims telephoned our house. He left a message on our answering machine because I was very sick in hospital at the time. Fr. Svet's words gave me great hope. I got to know Fr. Svet during my trips to Medjugorje; he is known as the 'Eyes of Christ' and is a very wise and Holy Franciscan priest. He has written several books about Medjugorje, and one of the first published in English. I will speak more about him later on. His words made me see my situation in a way that reassured me that God was close. Even though it was not an easy time, a time when I could have felt God was far away, very far away. Fr. Svet's words inspired me to call this book after some of those words 'In the Moments of God'. Here is the message he left for us.

"Hello. This is Father Svet's calling from Medjugorje, greetings to you all. I just want to say that I'm in my prayers with you. I know Ken is not doing very well. In your moments of concern, of hope and prayer. But, also in the moments of God. In the moment, that belongs to God alone. In the moment that God knows and controls. I'm with you in prayer. I'm with you in prayer and very

much greetings to you all, encouragement. This is a moment of faith where God blesses us all. Take care and feel safe that I'll call again. Bye now." Fr. Svet September 2000.

After listening to the message several times I began to reflect on his words and realised that they apply to everyone, and to everyone's life. We all have major events or moments in our lives when we ask ourselves 'why' and 'What is life all about?' Moments of God! After years of asking these questions myself, I had turned away from God and decided that I could cope better on my own. I could not understand why God had given me Cystic Fibrosis. I decided that God was not for me at the wise old age of fourteen.

God and His Blessed Mother are so loving, that they both let me choose my own path and do my own thing. That is God's gift of free will. Over the years I came to terms with the fact that I was different to others my own age because of my Cystic Fibrosis and was happy, or so I thought.

My book begins in 1981, the year the alleged apparitions in Medjugorje started. It follows my life and the many twists and turns it has taken up until now. These twists and turns are God's moments in my life and have taught me something new in each instance. You too may be experiencing your own moment of God and may indeed be wondering 'Why' and 'What is next for you?' I hope and pray that my story may help you in your moment of God. He is never far away, we just have to give Him time and be aware of Him throughout our day.

Chapter 1

1981

On June 24th, 1981 the story of Medjugorje began. I was a five-year-old Dublin boy waiting anxiously for my sixth birthday, which fell on the 27th. Finally some attention would be on me again, as my new baby brother Gary had been hogging all my parents attention and time. It was summer time and I was out playing games with my friends and big sister Lorna who was eight years of age at the time. So, I didn't envy Gary, as I knew that he needed Mam more than I did. Anyway Mam would be doing my physiotherapy later on in the evening, so I'd spend time with her on the good old therapy-thumper (a Simi-circular foam device that I'd lay across while Mam or Dad clapped my back, however it was also the best toy as a child, we found many uses for it. Mam always said they should be sold in toyshops for everyone).

You see I was born with Cystic Fibrosis 'CF', so this was part of my daily routine; my physio was done twice a day to clear mucus from my lungs. If it was not done the mucus would build up and cause bacteria and infections to develop in my lungs. CF is a genetic disorder that mainly affects the lungs and digestive system and is incurable. I was diagnosed when I was ten months old after having poor health since my birth. I have always known that I had CF for as long as I can remember. My parents were very honest with me and I understood CF as best as I could. There were times when I had many questions about why I had CF. Mam and Dad always tried to answer these questions as best they could. One answer I remember that reassured me was, 'God made you special'. That was good for me to hear when I was young and I still had the mind of a child. It was also good because I knew God created the whole world and that was impressive to a small child. At times I would even question who created God and where exactly did the universe actually end? It had to end some place? Right! My parents tried to answer my many questions as parents do, constantly reassuring me everything would be ok. Though at times I could see a puzzled look come across their faces. I came up with many questions that even God himself, may have to think hard about before answering.

Prayer time in our house as children was always at bedtime. Mam or Dad always said prayers with us as we settled down for the night. We would say the 'Our Father', 'Hail Mary' and God bless Mammy, Daddy, Lorna, Ken and Gary, and everyone we knew. Prayer time was kept simple for us. Sometimes we'd add other names of people who'd come to mind at prayer time.

Meanwhile in Yugoslavia, from June 24th, 1981 it was reported that six children had seen 'Gospa' (the Croatian word for Our Lady). The youngest of these children was Jakov, who had just turned ten years of age. He was two years older than my sister Lorna. The oldest of these children was sixteen. Altogether there were four girls and two boys. Vicka, Mirjana, Marija, Ivanka, Ivan and Jakov. Yugoslavia in 1981 was a communist country and the practice of religion was confined to inside churches, at times it was barely tolerated. So the government officials wanted quick answers to what was allegedly happening in this tiny village in this region of Herzegovina.

Once these sightings commenced large crowds began gathering each evening on the side of a hill called 'Podbrdo' in Bijakovici. The government feared these gatherings were of a political nature and wanted them stopped. They suspected that the local Franciscan order of priests in Medjugorje were the instigators of these happenings. After a number of days, news of these apparitions quickly spread throughout the region. The government made 'Podbrdo' (now known as the 'hill of apparitions' or 'apparition hill') off limits. It eventually forced the children away from the hill to where they found refuge in the local church. The parish priest, Fr Jozo Zovko, found it hard to believe these children. One day while alone in the church he asked God to enlighten him on the situation as he was finding it very difficult to comprehend what was going on with these children. Fr. Jozo then heard in an audible voice, he knew it was God, telling him to 'protect the children'. When he heard this voice he went directly to the church door. As he opened it, he saw the six children running toward him. They wanted help as the police where chasing them. Fr. Jozo hid the children in the rectory. While there, the children had an apparition of Our Lady. They asked Our Lady if they could have the apparition in the church the following day. Our Lady agreed and the following day the apparitions began to take place inside the Church of St. James. Many people had come to the village to witness these strange events. Fr. Jozo didn't want people running around the village looking for the visionaries. He decided to celebrate the rosary before and after Holy Mass and have everyone gather in the church each evening. This practice continues to this day over 30 years later.

One of Our Lady's first messages to the children was to say that, 'God exists'. Our Lady appeared in this small parish in the middle of Communist Yugoslavia to change the hearts of people throughout the world. She appeared to lead the world back to her Son, Jesus, and she continues to change the hearts of many people throughout the world today.

Chapter 2

Medgi What?

In 1989 the daily apparitions in Medjugorje continued, and it was in March that I first heard of Medjugorje. 'Medgi what?' was my first reaction. I was fourteen and my life as I knew it was changing. Mam and Dad were about to go to Medjugorje after a very difficult year for all the family.

Dad had Crohns Disease since 1977 and his health had deteriorated dramatically over the last year. In 1984 he had lost his faith in God because of his health and because of my Cystic Fibrosis. Dad decided God was not for him. 'How could God let a child suffer?' was his reasoning, so Dad stopped going to Holy Mass, except on special occasions. The classic 'Why Me God, Syndrome' as I call it, had set in. As well as that, in the last year Dad had walked out on the family twice and he began a relationship with another woman. This hurt all of us very much, especially Mam. At this time Mam was getting to know God better and had just finished a course that she had attended once a week in our church, St. Aengus's, which is a Dominican parish. This provided Mam with a great support network both from God and her new found friends.

Those days were strange, difficult and painful, but Mam reassured us that everything would be fine. Mam has great faith in God, and God graced Mam with great love and the ability to forgive. So it was, that she invited Dad home twice after he walked out on the family. The first time Dad came back the atmosphere in the house was very tense. Eventually Dad left again after a few weeks and hurt us all over again. I knew Mam's love for Dad was great, and this really hurt, much worse than the first time. But Mam forgave Dad again and in June 1988 she invited Dad back home again for the 'children's sake'. Relationships were very strained in the house, but we were all under one roof and that eased my mind.

Then just before Christmas 1988 Dad got very sick and was taken into hospital. His Crohns Disease had advanced and he needed to undergo major surgery. The operation was not a success and had to be repeated a week later on New Year's eve. After this operation the surgeon and doctors said that they'd done everything medically possible and that they could do any more for Dad. In their opinion Dad only had weeks to live. At the time, I didn't realise how sick Dad was, but I knew it was serious.

Dad was very ill; he had lost a lot of weight and was a very sickly grey colour. These events brought Mam and Dad closer than they had been in months. While recovering from his latest operation Dad spoke of his desire to go on holiday which we thought was wishful thinking on Dad's part. He desired to return to Yugoslavia, Mam and Dad had honeymooned there, in a place called Cavtat, which is close to Dubrovnik on the Adriatic Coast. Five years after their honeymoon they brought Lorna and myself on holiday there too, I was three years of age. However, for now this was only a dream for Dad as he lay in his hospital bed with nothing else to do but think. But God was listening to his wish.

At this time Dad was a professional singer, working in one of Dublin's major hotels, 'The Burlington Hotel'. He was a resident singer along with a band. And now because he was out of work the band decided to hold a benefit night to help the family financially. Mam and Dad were invited to this night which was held after Dad came out of hospital. Dad was still very sick and went reluctantly. The night was a great success, Dad even managed to sing one or two songs. The following day, Dad told Mam that a man he knew offered them both a pilgrimage to Medjugorje in Yugoslavia when Dad felt well enough to travel. Dad's dream of traveling to Yugoslavia would come true.

Mam had known about Medjugorje, having remembered reading an article about it in one of the newspapers a few years previously. She only remembered the name because Yugoslavia was so special to her and Dad. Mam tried to explain to us the little she remembered about the article. I was on my own journey and didn't really care about Medjugorje and what was alleged to be happening there. I was young and my interest in religion was fading rapidly.

Anyway, the man told Dad he would telephone at some stage during the day to make arrangements. When no phone call came Dad felt it was probably just a case of someone getting caught up in the moment. The following day however, the phone call arrived and all the arrangements were finalised. The week long trip was scheduled for April, only a few weeks away.

When the day came for their pilgrimage to Medjugorje, Lorna, Gary and myself stayed with our aunt, Hilary and our uncle Pat and our three cousins; Tom, Sue and Greg. We had a great time and looked forward to seeing Mam and Dad on their return.

Medjugorje was not as developed in 1989 as it is now. Communication by telephone was expensive and there where no mobile phones either. So we did not hear from Mam or Dad throughout the whole week.

Chapter 3

Returning Together

Finally their week in Medjugorje was over. A week is a long time when you're young. We didn't go to the airport to meet my parents; instead we went home to our home, while my uncle collected them. I don't remember the exact details of that evening, but I remember everyone gathered in our front room. There were a lot of our relatives in the house to welcome them home. I'll never forget the happiness in my parent's faces as the tried to tell us what they did for the week. Their eyes where bright and their smiles took over their faces as they stood there. They talked simultaneously and remained close to each other as they relayed their adventure. Dad was not walking hunched as he had been when he left; clearly something wonderful had happened in Medjugorje. After a while Lorna, then sixteen ran out of the room crying. Mam followed her out to the kitchen followed by Dad. After a few minutes I went out to see what was going on. When I got to the kitchen Mam was hugging Lorna and Dad was hugging the two of them. Lorna was crying because she'd never seen Mam and Dad so happy together. Soon I was crying and part of this big hug. God decided in all his wisdom and mercy to heal my Dad both spiritually and physically.

Over the next few months Dad got stronger physically and amazed his doctors. His consultant said 'Continue to do whatever your doing'. The doctors wanted to test

Dad after he told them what happened in Medjugorje. Eventually after Dad went for the tests, the doctors could find no trace of Crohns Disease. Dad was able to return to work after a number of weeks and life went back to normal. However Dad's healing caused me much soul searching and it eventually drove me further away from God. I was happy that Dad was feeling better but I was still sick, so I thought God was not for me, 'Why Me God, Syndrome' had struck again. I was angry at God and Jealous of Dad's healing. I didn't want to know about God and decided to walk away from Him. My friends would say, 'How can you not believe in God, your Dad was cured.!!!' I was young and thought I knew it all, and of course, there was no talking to me. I just didn't listen or want to hear it. I began to skip going to Mass and eventually stopped going, stopped praying. However, Mam continued to pray for all of us (Lorna, Gary and myself) and Dad continued with his conversion as they both began to try and live the messages of Medjugorje.

Chapter 4

Our Lady's Children's Hospital

As I start this chapter I think of the words 'I will never forget you my people, I have carved you in the palm of my hand'. God and Our Lady have been looking after me for years, but I only recognise this now. I was a patient in Our Lady's Children's Hospital in Crumlin, an area of Dublin since I was a small baby. My Mam and Dad were advised to bring me there just after I was diagnosed with Cystic Fibrosis at ten months old. They did, and my health improved greatly. I had spent months in another Dublin hospital that is now closed and at one point Mam and Dad were told I would not make it through the night. God then provided my first miracle. There is a longer story about this that I've told very few people, Fr. Svet from Medjugorje once told me, not to tell everyone about all of the special moments, 'hold some back for you', 'they are between you and God'. In this miracle, I believe that I was given the option to 'stay' or go 'back'. I chose to go back, it might have been God who gave me this option, I didn't see His face, but Padre Pio had a major hand with this miracle too.

I will give you the short version, the story goes that, I was very sick one day and my Mam and Dad were told I was not expected to make it through the night, I could not keep any of my food down and my infection was getting the better of me. So, Mam decided to place a Padre Pio prayer card with a third class relic under my pillow in my cot without anyone knowing. The next morning the doctors were amazed that I had survived the night. When Mam and Dad came into see me the next morning, the doctors told them how much I had improved during the night. At that time, 1970's no one could stay in hospital with patients, not even parents. The doctors could offer no explanation for my improvement, as they were sure I should have died during the night. Then Mam noticed a tiny piece of paper in my cot. When she investigated this piece of paper she could not find the prayer card with the relic of Padre Pio. I had eaten and digested the relic during the night and since then my health improved greatly. A few months after this I was transferred to Our Lady's Hospital Crumlin as an outpatient and was under the care of the Doctors there for all of my childhood into my teenage years.

Crumlin Hospital, as we called it, played a major part in my life, but not as much for me as other CF children. I mainly went there every three months for my outpatient's clinic. At the age of fourteen in 1990, I had my first ever hospital admission for a chest infection that required IV (intravenous) antibiotics. I spent two weeks in hospital on St. Michaels ward, the specialist Cystic Fibrosis ward. I got familiar with the hospital quickly but I didn't like being an inpatient much. Who does? My health had been really great up to this admission, although I was always small for my age. I was a skinny kid with blonde hair. Growing up I loved soccer and played for a local team, but because of my health I spent more time on the bench as a substitute. I could never understand why I was a sub so much; I was able to run around for hours-on-end playing soccer. The men running the club knew that I had CF so maybe that's why they didn't play me so often. Or else they thought I was rubbish, but I thought I was a good player. However, around the time of this hospital admission I stopped playing football and began skateboarding with my best friend Marc. We both played soccer for years on the same team and lived around the corner from each other. We started to skateboard with a few other friends and had great fun learning how to do different tricks. We became quite good and learned the latest moves. We had many a good time traveling around Dublin city skateboarding and going to competitions, only as spectators mind.

In August 1991, I ended up in hospital again. I had just turned sixteen and because of this my doctor wanted me to transfer over to St. Vincent's, an adult hospital in Elm Park, an area of Dublin. I didn't feel ready for this transfer. The fear of the unknown was a big factor in my reluctance to change hospitals. However, this way of thinking changed towards the end of my admission. One day I was talking to a teenage boy who was working in the hospital for the summer before he went to college. He asked me what year I was going into in school. I told him I was going into sixth year in secondary school. He taught I meant sixth class in primary school which would have made me 11 or 12 years of age in his eyes. I tried to convince him that I was sixteen but he would not believe me. So I made my mind up in that instance that I was changing over to the adult hospital as soon as it was possible. After this admission the plans were made for my transfer to St. Vincent's hospital later that year in November.

In November 1991, the daily apparitions of Medjugorje were now happening for over ten years, but only to four of the six visionaries now. I still had no interest in Medjugorje and was drifting further and further from God. God's Love for us is so patient. But in 1991, I could not have cared less, I was the centre of my world and that was all that mattered to me, I was getting more and more selfish.

So, the big day came for my first visit to St. Vincent's hospital to be shown the CF adult unit. I was a bit scared at first but when I got there my fears were eased. Everyone was very friendly and it didn't seem to be the bad place I had imagined. While there it was arranged for me to go into hospital for five days and do all kinds of tests to start my medical file. I think it was arranged for January or February, I can't remember exactly. The school year continued with me sitting my leaving certificate in June 1992, the last secondary school exams that decide what college you go to, if indeed you apply for college. I hadn't applied for college; I had no real interest in going. I was never very good at studying, and fortunately God has blessed me with a good memory, so I remembered enough to pass my exams. I was shocked when I got my results, I was sure I had failed at least two subjects, but God had provided me with another miracle. I was not yet seventeen and had finished school and my final exams. I hadn't a clue what I wanted to do after school, so I decided to take a year off. Being so young and deciding what to do for the rest of my life seemed a bit stupid to me because of my CF. All I could see for my future was me dying young, so I had no motivation or hope. My life didn't make sense to me.

Chapter 5

Spread the Good News

In 1992 dad's health was very good but he was faced with another problem, work! He was offered redundancy from the hotel as things were changing in the hotel regarding their entertainment arrangements. Dad had several months to decide what to do before he was to finish in the hotel. Mam suggested he record a song called 'Let me live' that he had sang years before at a song contest. While in Medjugorje in 1989 Dad had promised Our Lady that he'd do something when he got home in thanksgiving for his healing, but didn't know what. While in Medjugorje, some American pilgrims prayed for an end to abortion, as a bill was about to be passed in America and these prayers were much needed to end this awful act on the unborn child. So with this in mind Dad began to try and get money together to record the song. A friend of his decided to invest the money for the song. While getting the cost of recording the song, they found it would cost the same to record an album rather than the one song. So they decided to record an album. A list of songs was drawn up, all popular easy listening songs. When the album was finished and ready to be released a problem arose with 'Let Me Live'. A man-made problem that had no suitable answer, so the album was released without 'Let Me Live', the original song and inspiration behind the album. Strange but true! But God and Our Lady were already busy remedying this situation.

Dad was not satisfied with this outcome and wanted to do more with the song. This desire led him to America and there he met several people without any success in both Chicago and Boston. Dad was then given the name of Martin Henry, an Irish record distributor. They met in a Boston hotel, and after hearing the song twice on a personal stereo Martin decided he'd do whatever he could to help. 'People have to hear this song!' he said. After this meeting it was decided an album of religious songs should be recorded rather than a single. So 'Let Me Live' was now the working title of this new album. It was released in Ireland and in America. Being a distributor Martin had many contacts and the album was quickly sent out to various customers. Dad was invited to speak and sing at a Marian Conference in California in November 1992. This invitation came about after he met an American pilgrim in Medjugorje, while Dad was working making a documentary about Medjugorje, with a video production company that Dad and three others set up called 'Quatro Vision'.

Back in Dublin, after that conference in California it was time for a decision regarding work in the hotel. After his appearance in California, Dad was now getting offers to speak and sing at other conferences around the U.S.A. Mam and Dad spoke and prayed about it and felt that God and Our Lady were going to look after the family. So Dad accepted the redundancy offer and began to put his trust in God and whatever God had planned for him. Meanwhile, the offers to go back to the U.S.A waited a decision. Dad decided to work for God, and to this day has travelled the world several times spreading the Good News of the Kingdom of God.

Chapter 6

My Journey Continues

While Dad began his work with the Lord, the rest of the family continued on as normal with Mam at home for our every need. In 1993 after my year off, I decided to go to college and get a diploma in computer studies. I did very well on the course and passed my exams with good grades. I learned new skills, one of which was how to type on a typewriter. At the time I wondered why would I need to know how to type? Now as I am writing this, I know why! However, my health worsened in this year. Due to my early starts in the morning I neglected my health by not taking some of my medication, mainly the two through my nebuliser. They are vital to my good health. A nebuliser is a device used to administer medication in the form of a mist inhaled into the lungs. As a result of this I had to go on my 'back-up' medication (a course of stronger antibiotics and steroids) to fight an infection. This would be successful for another few weeks. But, my health would gradually deteriorate again without me even realising how bad I was getting.

In July 1994 I went to America on holiday for the first time with my parents and Gary. I had always had a desire to see America ever since I was child. I grew up seeing so much of it on television and movies. Now I was getting this opportunity to see America and I was extremely excited about our holiday. Lorna was in already Memphis, America for the summer visiting friends and working. We flew to Boston and stayed in

Martin (Mattie) Henry's house south of the city centre. We stayed there a few days before staying at Martin's brother Noels' home. Noel and his family had gone to Medjugorje and Ireland on a pilgrimage. They kindly gave us the use of their home. We spent three weeks in America and had a great time. The Henry family were the perfect hosts. Mattie, Mary, and their children Marty and Erin showed us the sights that made their city so wonderful. Mattie and his family are great friends and like family now. The holiday was very special and left me with many memories. One thing I'll never forget however, was the humidity. I was not feeling too good and the heat and humidity didn't help me at all. We Irish are not build for that kind of heat.

When I got back to Dublin I was in poor health and after a few weeks I knew I had to go into hospital. I really didn't want to go to hospital because I had tickets to a rock concert the following day. The concert featured an up-and-coming band called, 'Oasis'. I'd read about them and they were tipped to be the next big thing! My body was exhausted, I had an extremely high temperature as my body fought this infection and I had to stay in hospital. I was not very happy with this outcome and reluctantly stayed in hospital and subsequently missed the concert. So as my two cousins Olivia and Carla went to the concert the following evening I spent my evening in St. Paul's ward beginning a two-week admission. However, this disappointment soon turned to joy. Without me knowing anything, my aunt Rita, Olivia and Carla's mother, felt terrible for me and telephoned the venue of the rock concert and tried to get me the bands' autograph. She explained what had happened to me, and she was told to come to the venue in the afternoon before the concert to collect something for me. After collecting the gift she came into the hospital and handed me a signed T-shirt by all the members of the band. I was delighted and this made up for the disappointment of missing the concert. Thanks Rita, I still remember this as though it was yesterday.!!

This latest hospital admission was only my fourth in nineteen years, and I wasn't a very good patient. I was told I'd have to stay in hospital for two weeks. I got to know the nurses and other CF patients who where admitted around the same time. St. Vincent's hospital has Ireland's largest adult CF clinic. Many people with CF attended from all over Ireland and have to travel great distances for their appointments and admissions, so I guess I was lucky living in Dublin. During this admission I learnt my lesson with regards taking my medication properly. After my previous admission two years earlier I was not so good at taking my medication, especially my nebuliser. This is the most important of all my medications and I was only taking it every now and then when I should have been taking it twice a day. But seeing other patients sicker than I was, made me think long and hard about my own life. I also heard about other people with CF whom I shared previous admissions with who had passed away. So I really began to think about changing my ways and becoming compliant with my doctor's treatment.

I got out of hospital after the two weeks and began to take my medication properly. Life soon got back on track. I then started to look after my grandmother,

'Nana Kathleen' as we all called her, in the afternoons. She could no longer be left on her own. She was almost 80 years of age and was slowing down in mobility because of her arthritis. While minding her I began to teach myself guitar, I wanted to be the next Noel Gallagher of Oasis. My cousin Carla had a guitar in the house that did not see much daylight. So I slowly began to teach myself. It was ideal, because I'd let Nana say her prayers while I practiced guitar. After months I was able to play some Oasis and Beatles songs, badly. I thought I was great. I looked after Nana for about three years, after that time I stopped visiting her everyday. Her health deteriorated and the family members took turns caring for her throughout the week.

In these three years I went to America five times and got to know Mattie and his family really well and learned a lot from them, especially about living in the way of prayer. Even though I still had no interest in God and thought they wasted their time, with all that praying. Every time I was with them they'd invite me to pray with them, I often wondered why Mattie kept asking me to join in with them. I often spoke to Mattie about his faith and Mattie was always gentle with me and explained it in a way that made me respect him for his beliefs. But I always told him God was not for me.

I will never forget the month I spent with them in December of 1995. It was during this time that I really got to know the Henry Family. Mattie and Myself got on really well with one another and we had such a good laugh. During my time there it snowed and snowed so much. I got a taste of shoveling the car out of the drive way. I have to say I did not last too long at any of my attempts. I even did a bit of Christmas shopping with Mattie and I tried on a lovely woman's coat. Mattie figured I was about Mary's height and told, I mean asked me to try it on. We had such a laugh.

Mattie and Mary inspired me everyday with their faith, even though as I said, I had no interest in God. They lived such a prayerful life in and around their daly routines. Everyday while I was in their home Mattie's alarm would go off a 3pm. He would then call Mary and invite me to pray with them. I would decline and then listen to them pray what I thought was the most depressing prayer I'd ever heard. They seemed to make it sound even more depressing than the words, 'for the sake of His sorrowful passion, have mercy on us and on the whole world'. Depressing as it sounded, it stuck in my mind and I've still not forgotten their prayer life. A truly inspirational witness of faithfulness to God.

Chapter 7

Show Me on Friday

In June 1997, Mam and Dad celebrated 25 years of married life. Mam does not like flying and Dad had been invited to Hawaii, he wanted Mam travel with him for their anniversary. Mam said there was no way she would fly all that distance. She said 'The only place I'll fly to is Medjugorje,'. So Dad agreed and they booked to go for a week. Dad had been back to Medjugorje twice since 1989, but Mam had not been back and was really looking forward to it. Gary and myself stayed at home on our own while they went, Lorna was in Germany for the summer with her boyfriend Cyrelle. The week passed by quickly and we went to the airport with my aunt Rita and her friend Margaret to collect them, it was on June 17th the day of their wedding anniversary. When I saw them both, they were so happy and looked great after their week in the sunshine. Seeing them reminded me of the time they returned home in 1989, which, I'd nearly forgotten about. Their eyes were bright and seemed to dance with delight. They introduced us to their new friends that they had shared their week with; they too seemed full of this joy and happiness. Something happened in my heart at that moment, I thought to myself and only to myself, maybe I'll go to Medjugorje someday. I didn't mention this thought I'd had to anyone.

Dad had an up-coming trip to America and wanted Mam to travel with him. On the trip home from Medjugorje on the Tuesday Mam decided she would go if Gary and myself went too. So the following Saturday morning we all flew to America.

Since my first trip to America three years previous Mam, Dad, Mattie and Mary in Boston had tried to persuade me to go to Medjugorje, but I kept saying 'nothing is happening over there' and to remember that I didn't believe in God. This fact, never stopped them asking me though. So, one afternoon while having lunch in Mattie and Mary's kitchen, Mam said to me, "Ken, would you not go to Medjugorje with Mattie?" Mattie was due travel on a pilgrimage to Medjugorje at the end of July. To all their amazement I agreed by saying "Yes Sure, what harm can a week do". They where so shocked that Dad jumped from his seat and telephoned Ireland immediately and booked my place on the pilgrimage. I think we were all shocked including me that I said I'd travel.

Back at home after America the time for my pilgrimage to Medjugorje was approaching, too quick for my liking. Then came my chance of a way out..!! The Saturday before departure, Dad telephoned me when I was at my Nana Kathleen's house. He told me that Mattie was sick and could not travel, on his doctor's orders. Dad had expected me to pull out of the pilgrimage, and didn't mind if I did. But I instantly said that I'd go anyway. The pilgrimage was only for a week and I knew a few people going from America anyway. My response amazed him and surprised me too.

The morning of departure Tuesday July 22nd, 1997, came all too quickly. The night before I had joked with neighbours and relations that I would be holding a healing service on my return the following week. That's how much of a joke I took Religion..!! I was not buying into this 'Religion' thing at all. At the Airport I joked with Gary, who was beginning to think like me, "How do I bless myself". In the cafe before going through to the departure gate Mam handed me wooden Rosary beads, and said, "You'll need these". "Yeah, right", I replied and shoved them into my pocket before anyone saw them. I went through the departure gate and so began my pilgrimage. Mattie's sister in-law Winnie was on the trip with her daughter, Colleen, who took Mattie's place. Winnie introduced me to some of her friends, my fellow pilgrims whose names I'd forgotten almost instantly. Except for Sean, one of the few men I had noticed when I was being introduced to everyone.

On the plane I sat alone at a window seat, as the plane was not full. I was happy to do so, away from these religious nuts, was my thinking. There was a group of teenage girls from Belfast, Northern Ireland and their helpers sitting nearby. The flight was smooth and I looked in awe as we flew over the Alps. After nearly two and half-hours I got my first glimpse of the Croatian coastline. What a sight it was to behold with the many islands and the sunshine glistening on the Adriatic Sea. This is more like it, I thought to myself. Maybe the week wouldn't be so bad after all. When the plane touched down in Split airport and came to a halt, steps were driven over to the plane and the doors where opened. As I stepped out into the warm air the heat of the sun felt great. It was evening time and still great heat coming from the sun. We then got on the buses that brought us to the terminal building. We made our way through immigration and I got my passport stamped by an unfriendly looking airport official. He stared at me with a suspicious look in his eyes. When I collected my bag and guitar, I made my way out of the airport and to the bus that our group was assigned. When all the groups boarded their buses and everyone was counted, it was time to leave for Medjugorje.

Our guide on the bus to Medjugorje was an Irish young man called Philip. Incidentally, he is a neighbour of mine at home. His mother Patricia and brother Ed were also on the pilgrimage. Although they lived near me I didn't know any of them that well. The journey to Medjugorje is a three-hour drive from Split airport. I found myself a seat on my own down the back of the bus. All troublemakers head for the back of the bus, especially troublemakers on a pilgrimage I thought to myself. I'd noticed everyone seemed to be paired off with someone and chatting away as we waited to depart. This is when I began to regret coming on my own, I began to wonder what I was doing with a group who'd been together for several days already traveling around Ireland. What had I done?, I thought as the buses pulled away, but, there was no turning back now. I settled down for the journey to Medjugorje and starred out the window.

After several minutes on the road, Philip switched on a microphone at the front of the bus and welcomed us all. He then proceeded to tell us what was scheduled for the week. I began to think "Oh No! Really, What have I let myself in for?" Philip then said that Friday was the feast of St. James and it is a very special feast day in Medjugorje because St. James is the patron saint of Pilgrims. This caught my attention because the little I did know about Medjugorje was that St James is the name of the Church. I didn't know much of the details surrounding the alleged apparitions, only that Our Lady had supposedly appeared to six children. That's all I knew about Medjugorje. So, on hearing that Friday was the Feast of St. James I said to myself, 'well if there is any thing happening here, then show me on Friday'. I was challenging Our Lady to see if she did exist. I say 'Our Lady' now as I write this but at the time I didn't know who or what I was challenging. Remember I had stopped believing in God eight years before.

When Philip finished outlining our schedule for the rest of the week he said now we'll say the rosary for a safe journey and for a good pilgrimage. 'Here we go', I thought and I then switched my attention back to what was outside the bus window and wished I'd brought my personal stereo. I looked at the passing countryside before we came to the Adriatic Coastline I was fascinated by the many small little villages we passed. Watching the sun setting on the Adriatic coast was the most spectacular thing I'd seen in years. The colours' were beautiful and some on the bus tried to capture the moment on camera, it truly was magnificent.

When the bus left the Adriatic coast, the scenery was not as spectacular so I began to take an interest in my fellow pilgrims. Mainly to see if there was anyone else my own age or close to it, apart from Colleen, Winnie's daughter. I didn't notice anyone at first but somewhere along the way I noticed a girl around my own age, in her early twenties. A very good-looking girl I thought to myself, maybe the week won't be too bad after all. Looking at it now, Our Lady knew exactly how to get me interested in Medjugorje. I guessed this girl was with her mother and figured she was probably dragged here too, why else would someone so young be here I thought. Sometimes I think too much. We arrived in Medjugorje at about 10pm. The bus driver drove towards the church, and there it was, with her twin towers lit up in the night-sky, St James Parish Church. Just like in the home video Mam and Dad made some weeks before on their trip. After stopping at the front of the church briefly, the bus started up again and made its way back to where we'd come from. The bus stopped at the house where we'd be staying. We were met by a woman called Stanka, her husband and their eldest son. Stanka welcomed us with a smile that suggested she'd known us for years, very friendly. We got our bags from the bus and then dragged them up the long marble driveway to the front of the house. Philip began to read out who'd be sharing rooms before we entered the house. Philip then said, "Ken I hope you don't mind, you'll be sharing with Fr. Joe". I sarcastically thought to myself "this is just getting better". That was my initial reaction but Fr. Joe is a lovely priest who I'd met in America and I was happy enough to share with him. I hoped he wouldn't mind sharing with me. I imagine God does things for a reason and has a great laugh sometimes with his reasons. Anyway I thought Fr. Joe will not force religion down my throat, and he didn't. We were told just to drop our bags in our rooms as Stanka had prepared supper for us after our long journey. Afterwards, I walked down to the church with Fr. Joe and a few others. The church was locked for the evening, so we walked around the church grounds. While walking I noticed that there was the strange phenomenon of the birds chirping and singing even though it was close to midnight. I have never heard anything like it before at home.

The weather on Wednesday and Thursday was extremely hot. I went to mass on Wednesday morning simply because I didn't want to stay alone in my room. On arrival in our room Tuesday night, I'd noticed we had a balcony, maybe a chance to sunbathe I thought. Unfortunately I discovered this balcony was well shaded all day so that option was knocked on the head. Early on Thursday morning we went up Podbrdo, or Apparition Hill, as it is now known. At the base of the hill we heard the story of Medjugorje during the first days of the apparitions back in 1981. We heard from another of our guides, Jozo, He was roughly the same age as the visionaries. He gave his testimony of the early days of the apparitions. We then made our way up the hill stopping at each of the plaques depicting the Joyful Mysteries of the Rosary to pray. Mysteries? I didn't know there were any..!!, that's how little I knew. I was making my way up the hill not really paying attention to the prayers. At the site of the apparitions everyone found a rock to sit and pray. Everyone seemed deep in prayer or in thought. I was definitely not praying. I was wondering 'What on earth I was doing here'. Here I was, in the middle of nowhere in a foreign country, up a mountain looking at a church off in the distance. It was 9am and the sun was blazing, almost unbearable heat plus it was only early into my week here. At that moment I felt I had made a big mistake in coming to Medjugorje. It was going to be a very long week. However, one good thing that happened earlier that morning, Fr Joe introduced me to the girl from the bus at breakfast, her name is Sims.

Friday July 25th, the Feast of St James started normally enough for Medjugorje with an early breakfast. The group from our house were going to a place called the Blue Cross before mass. As we walked to the Blue Cross, Philip showed us the spot on the hill where the visionaries first saw Our Lady. After this we made our way up the small rocky incline to the Blue Cross, there was a Statue of Our Lady at the foot of the blue cross. I then found myself a rock to sit on and tried to get comfortable, but to no avail, so I found a small piece of wood and balanced it on two rocks to make a seat. Slightly better than a rock. I was then happy to see Sims make her way towards me and sit next to me. When everyone found a place Philip began to tell us about the Blue Cross and why it was such a special place to pray. He told us that in the early days of the apparitions in 1981, Our Lady appeared to the children in this spot when the police were chasing them. They were very frightened as they ran, and when they got to this spot, Our Lady appeared to them. They all fell to their knees and began praying with Our Lady. The police, who were very close behind, did not see or hear the children praying when they came and passed by still searching. Our Lady had protected the children from the police. To this day, Ivan and his prayer group hold prayer meetings once or twice a week there. During these prayer meetings Ivan has an apparition with Our Lady who is guiding and helping the prayer group. Philip said the Blue Cross is very special and the site of many a spiritual healing. I began to think about Medjugorje and the visionaries. I began to think, 'maybe' and 'what if', and I began to listen to what was being said. Philip then related a story of one such spiritual conversion, healing. The story was about two couples that had come to Medjugorje from one of the holiday coastal resorts. They were on holiday from England. One of these couples had lost a son in a car crash the previous year. The husband could not accept his son's death, and he'd lost all faith in God. They had to remove all photographs of their son that were on display in their house as the husband could not bear to look at his son's picture. His loss was too painful and the photographs brought back memories of the days surrounding his beloved son's death. The husband's behaviour and grief was putting a terrible strain on his relationship with his wife. They came on holiday to try and heal their relationship. They arrived in Medjugorje early one afternoon, on a day when the rain hadn't stopped for hours and did not look like it was going to anytime soon. They decided to get some lunch before they looked around the shrine. As they were finishing their lunch, Philip entered the restaurant rounding up some of his Irish pilgrims. The Irish pilgrims were going to the Blue Cross. Philip told these couples from England to come when they were ready, thinking they were part of his group. One of the women explained that they were only there for the day. Philip told them that they were more than welcome to join the group anyway. The couples decided to come along with the group. During

Philip's talk at the Blue Cross, he spoke of Our Lady and God's great love for us all. He spoke of the motherly love Our Lady has for all of us and how she wants all our past hurts and worries. She promises to take them away, just give them to her and she'll accept them with her Motherly Love. When Philip finished he told the group he'd let them have some time on their own. Philip was not too well at the time and the rain continued to pour down. He went back to his car and waited until he'd seen the entire group come down and make their way back to the village. He noticed the last people down were these two couples. The husband who had lost his son had a wonderful spiritual conversion and a complete change of heart. Philip only found out this man's story a year later when he met the same couple in the west of Ireland while on holiday. At the time in Medjugorje Philip didn't know anything about their story but he had, realised something amazing had happened to this man. He told us that he could see a physical change in the husbands face when he came down from the Blue Cross that rainy afternoon.

As Philip relayed this story I could feel tears well up in my eyes. I tried to fight them but they slowly trickled down my cheeks. Although this story was not like my own situation, I could identify with certain parts. The atmosphere at my home was very tense for a few months before my Dad got sick in 1988 and I was feeling the same way as this man was about God; 'how could God do this to me?' Memories surfaced in my mind that I'd not thought about in years. After wiping away my tears, Philip invited Fr. Joe to give a reflection. Fr. Joe began to speak about pilgrimage and how each one of us was led to Medjugorje whether we knew it yet or not. Our Lady invited everyone here to meet her Son. I began to think about what Fr. Joe was saying. He spoke of opening your heart to prayer and of telling Our Lady your hurts. She would take them from you. He encouraged us to let God in to our hearts. At this point those tears I thought I'd dealt with came back. This time I didn't care who was looking at me. The tears streamed out of my eyes and rolled down my cheeks. Some made their way into my mouth and, I could taste the salt of my own tears. Extremely salty in my case, as people with CF produce far more salt than others do. As I cried I experienced a real sadness in my heart, I somehow knew that God existed, and just for one moment I had felt His sadness; the sadness God has felt for so long, by me not believing in him. This sadness passed instantly and I felt a real joy, it's as though I received a new heart. No, it was more than that, not even a new heart. I imagined my heart was more like the petals of a flower opening to let the sun in and help it grow. I felt my heart was opening and ready to grow. Ready to blossom. At this point Sims put her arm around me and gently rubbed my back, like a mother does with her infant. She didn't say anything; the moment didn't need any words. Our Lady had placed Sims there to comfort me in this moment. I felt great. Even though I was still crying, I realised that God had made me exactly as He planned, and me having CF was a part of His plan for my life. Not the mistake I'd thought He'd made when He created me. I accepted God's unconditional love for me and began to love myself and accept my CF as a gift from God. I felt a great weight had been lifted off my shoulders. I know it is a cliché but that's why they are cliché's. That's what it felt like to me and it is the easiest way I can describe how I felt. When Fr. Joe had finished his reflection we sat in silence and could leave any time we wanted. I heard other people cry too; God touched many more in some way that morning. After a few minutes I made my way down on my own and waited for some of the others to come down. Philip had said he would give a few of us a lift back. A while later he came down with Sims and Colleen. He then drove us back to the village. On the way Philip stopped his car outside a house and said he'd be back in a minute. He was gone for a long time and we were getting very hot while waiting. We got out of the car for fresh air because it was too hot. The three of us chatted about all kinds of things, but not about what had happened at the Blue Cross. Sims had asked me if I was all right when she first came down from the Blue Cross. I said I was fine. She didn't ask me why or what had happened to me. I'm sure she knew something very personal was happening to me. I'm glad she didn't ask because at that moment, I don't think I could have explained what was going on in my Heart. After about three quarters of an hour waiting, Philip came out of the house and apologised to us for making us wait and said he'd buy us lunch. We stopped at Coco's one of the restaurants near St. James' church. While chatting Philip asked Sims about her unusual name. She explained that Sims was her second name, and that she and her mother shared the same first name. So to avoid confusion she was called Sims. I didn't want to ask Sims this when I first heard her name; I thought she probably gets asked about it all the time. But she didn't mind explaining. After lunch we went back to the house for a choir practice. I had said earlier that I would help by playing my guitar. Fr. Joe was celebrating the Holy Mass the following morning. We decided to rehearse outdoors in front of our house. While we were waiting to begin rehearsing Winnie asked me how I was doing. I just started crying and said that I was wonderful. She gave me a big hug as I cried. I was beginning to have all these new thoughts and feeling about Medjugorje and God. The emotions and tears were flowing out of me at every opportunity. It was funny for someone who didn't want to continue with the pilgrimage 24 hours earlier, I was now practicing with the choir for Holy Mass. God must laugh at us sometimes, especially me. He works many miracles and wonders.

Just before dinner Fr. Joe asked me if he could have a word in our room. Fr. Joe asked me if I would like to attend an apparition with Ivan one of the visionaries. Fr. Joe was invited and could bring a few others. As he asked me, I suddenly remembered what I'd said on the bus "show me on Friday". Today was Friday and all these things were happening to me. I said yes to his invitation not telling him what had happened to me earlier at the Blue Cross. After dinner we made our way down to the Adoration Chapel beside the church where the apparition would take place. When we went in Ivan was briefly introduced to us. Ivan asked two Irish priests to lead the Joyful and Sorrowful mysteries of the Rosary. The prayers started at 6pm; there were only about thirteen or so other people present in the Adoration Chapel. I knelt down with very mixed emotions ranging from absolute terror to total delight. I was delighted to be present at an apparition but terrified

I would see something. If Our Lady was about to appear what would she think of me? I was not praying and all these other thoughts were flying around my mind. I knelt down and tried to pray and think of people who had asked me to pray for them back home. As I tried to pray I became aware of a insect making noise, a cricket, had somehow gotten into the Adoration Chapel. The noise it made completely distracted me, so I tried harder to pray. In the meantime the Irish priests must have been feeling nervous too because they had both finished praying their mysteries at speed. Ivan had to ask another priest to say the Glorious mystery of the Rosary. Then the time approached for the apparition. Ivan made his way to the front of the chapel and knelt down. I peered around the person in front of me to get a better look. Then I realised what was about to happen and bowed my head. I thought if Our Lady appeared I didn't want her to see me not praying. I was in a cold sweat at this stage and kept my head down. With that the apparition started as Ivan's voice was no longer audible. I could feel my heart pounding away. Then I noticed that the cricket had stopped making noise and a silence filled the room. A silence that seemed to put pressure on my ears, I thought this was very strange. I then became curious to see what was going on before me, so I looked up. To my relief I did not see Our Lady. What I did see was Ivan kneeling down, head tilted looking upward and his head would nod up and down as if he was saying yes to someone. It was only then I thought 'Oh my goodness, the Mother of God is present and she can see me with my mouth open, not praying'. So I put my head down and started to pray even though I didn't know what praying really meant. I thought of many people who had asked for prayers and for others I hadn't seen in years, they would pop into my mind and thoughts. When the apparition finished the cricket began making noise again. I couldn't believe it.

When I was leaving the chapel Ivan pointed at my t-shirt and said "Ah Revolution". I was wearing a New England Revolution soccer jersey from the U.S.A. Ivan recognised it as he lives in Boston in the winter months as his wife is American. Little did he know the revolution that was taking place in my heart or maybe he did. After all he was just talking and praying with Our Lady. Outside, while talking to others who where present for the apparition, I asked if the cricket had distracted anyone else. They said 'what cricket?' When I explained about the cricket they said didn't hear anything. Surely I couldn't have imagined it, the noise was far too loud and real. Again I thought of what I said on the bus "show me on Friday". Our Lady was surely showing me. I just had to get the plank out of my own eye, and see. This 'Doubting Thomas' was starting to believe (and Thomas, is my middle name). I then made my way over to a bench outside at the back of the church. I sat down to get my head around what had just happened. Then I became aware of the great faith of the congregation inside the church. A hymn was being sung by everyone in the congregation with great feeling and broadcast on the outside speakers. I then thought everyone in the church would give anything to be where I had just been and I thanked Our Lady for that wonderful gift. I felt very happy and was shaking with the enormity of what happened. Later that evening I sat chatting and laughing outside with Sean, Sims and a few others. It was a relaxing way to end a wonderful day.

After Friday, the rest of the week was just a joy. I now wished I could stay longer. I no longer had the desire to go home as I had on Thursday. Over the next few days we visited the Cenacolo Community, a community of ex-addicts who live, work and pray together. While at the Community I was very impressed with their testimonies, the love they had for Jesus and Our Lady and each other was incredible. One young man, John Paul, had a joyous way about him. He seemed to be bursting with love, his eyes sparkled with brightness. His joy was infectious and one could not help but smile while listening to him. We also went up Mount Krizivac called 'Cross Mountain', and a few of us decided to spend the night up there. I couldn't make it to the top, as we did not stop at any of the Stations of the Cross. I was exhausted by the time we got between the tenth and eleventh station. So I stayed where I was with another girl Nancy who said she'd keep me company. Before we settled for the night she asked me if we'd say the Rosary together. I declined the offer and said I was tired. But to be honest at the time I didn't know how to pray the rosary and felt terrible. I should have said so and told her the truth. When we did settle down on our rocky beds it was about midnight. Pilgrims made their way up and down the mountain all night. This amazed me. I woke every hour until 5am when I decided to stop trying to sleep. As I sat there looking at the valley below, Fr. Slavko Barbaric a Franciscan priest based in Medjugorje made his way up the mountain, as I later found out he did most mornings. Nancy and myself had planned to watch the sunrise, but clouds rolled in and blocked our view. However, we did get some spectacular photographs of the sun's rays breaking through the clouds and shinning on little clusters of houses in the valley. The rest of our group had planned to meet us on the mountain. They got to where we were at around 8am. I decided to stay with our bags as the group and Nancy went to the top of the mountain. I was so tired that I had no desire at that time to see the top of the mountain. So I waited until they came down and made my way down with them in time for Holy Mass.

After lunch I was making my way back to our house when I met Sean and Sims. They just had lunch with Mary an Irish Girl whom they got friendly with and were planning on going to a local waterfall for the afternoon. They asked if I would like to go with them. I thought I could do with a break from all this religion, which I had all these new feelings for. I wanted to spend sometime away from it because it was all so new. I had thought I was happy with my life before Medjugorje. Now after Friday I had a different happiness, which I realise is God's love. I hoped that I could hold on to it when I got home. For now I needed to take a step back and get away from Medjugorje

We met Mary and two other Irish girls in front of their house and got a taxi. The six of us squashed in and headed for the waterfall. It was about 25 minutes away and we arranged to get the same taxi back later in the afternoon. At the waterfall we made our way down an embankment to the shores of the water. We crossed the river on a narrow plank of wood that led to where everyone else was. The area was crowded with local people all cooling off in the water and relaxing on this very hot summer afternoon. It's never that hot in Ireland. The waterfall was beautiful, and the water had hidden dangers; strong undercurrents in the water that have claimed the lives of people in the past. We were warned and told to be very careful. We found a spot among the crowds and settled down for a relaxing afternoon. During the afternoon I got talking to Sims alone close to the water's edge, I asked her how she had ended up in Medjugorje. She told me a bit about herself and the circumstances that led her to Medjugorje. She revealed that she'd felt Our Lady's love for her on the Thursday as she knelt and prayed before the beautiful statue of Our Lady in the church. She said she understood what was going on inside my heart when she gave me that little hug at the Blue Cross. I then told her how I'd ended up in Medjugorje and how I felt now. We were both very happy for each other and agreed in the fact that we were in Medjugorje for a reason and a part of God's great Master plan. It seemed that our group had all been hand picked to be with each other. Our Lady brought people together in our group that could help and keep us safe on our pilgrimage. For me there was a doctor and physiotherapist, people that could help me if I needed them. It also gave us something to talk about regarding my Cystic Fibrosis. After a number of hours of relaxing it was soon time to leave the waterfall and make our way back up the embankment for our taxi. We posed for a few photographs as we waited. Our taxi driver came and we headed back to Medjugorje in time for dinner.

On Monday July 28th, I went to mass alone as I slept late. As I got to the church Holy Mass was just starting. The church was crowded so I stayed standing at the back. The mass was lovely and I began to think about the real meaning of mass. The priest in his homily seemed to answer my questions and this made me think more. I now knew in my heart that Our Lady the Mother of God was appearing in Medjugorje, and that God really existed. I knew that I had a lot to learn and to change about myself. Then during Holy Mass a wonderful thing happened to me after Holy Communion. After I received Jesus in the communion host I knelt down to pray and the choir began to sing 'As I Kneel Before You', as I listened to the words they seemed to sum up exactly how I was feeling at that moment. I started to cry and cried until I left the church. My pilgrimage was coming to an end and I had realised in the last few days that God loved me no matter what. I knew now that he had not made a mistake when He created me. My Cystic Fibrosis was the very thing that caused me to turn my back on Him and walk away as a 14 year old boy. Now, I'd experienced a Love that changed my heart in an instance. For so long I had pushed him away thinking he was far away and then I denied His existence, but that had all changed in a few days of pilgrimage. I realised He is the one who got me to where I am. Now I felt that He was happy because I now know of His unconditional love for me and everyone else in the world. In His time, God will teach and reveal to you why He created you and why you are His masterpiece. It helps if we take the time to ask Him to reveal His love to us. He is waiting and wants us to come to him. All one has to do is open their heart and listen to God in silence. God's love for us is bigger than the universe. As I cried in the church I felt my life fell into place or I fell into place with my life. I thanked Jesus for his sacrifice on the Cross at Calvary and the gift of Our Lady's apparitions in Medjugorje.

In the church that morning I felt as if I had made my Holy Confirmation and received the seven gifts of the Holy Spirit. I felt my spirit rejuvenated beyond anything I had ever experienced before. Medjugorje is a special place where Heaven and Earth meet. I thanked God for my Parents, my siblings Lorna and Gary. I also thanked God for all of my family and friends. Now I had new friends to be thankful for, especially Sean and Sims. We had a great time during those last few days laughing, crying, talking, listening, praying and living in harmony on our pilgrimage. Outside the church after mass and still crying I met Sims, She looked at me and embraced me. We then made our way around to the dome at the back of the church for our final meeting about going home. As we sat facing Mt. Krizivac, it only seemed like we'd arrived the day before. Philip started the meeting with a prayer. After the prayer he gave us instructions of our departure the following day. Philip then gave a reflection about a song he'd heard which seemed to sum up how he felt on his first visit to Medjugorje. Philip said that while in Medjugorje he grew and learned a lot about who he was and about who God is. He seemed to say exactly how I was feeling earlier and I began to cry again. I was very joyful and happy that I experienced Gods love, but I also felt a small amount of sadness because I was leaving Medjugorje. I could see tears rolling down Sims cheeks too. Our Lady had touched our hearts in ways we never knew possible. Nothing is impossible to God.

Later that night as I lay on my bed I began to look forward to going home. I was excited about going home to tell everyone how I got on. It was as if I had received a big secret and was bursting to tell everyone. The only problem was that everyone in Medjugorje seemed to know this secret. I felt I was the last to know. Everyone seemed to have this joy and happiness. It was the same Joy and happiness that my Mam and Dad had when they returned home from Medjugorje in 1989 and in June just past.

Tuesday July 29th, 1997 I got up early and finished packing my bag. After breakfast and with all our suitcases downstairs ready for collection I went down to my final Mass in St. James' church with Sims. As we walked and talked we promised each other that we would try and keep in the tears today, because if we started crying today it would be too hard to leave Medjugorje. The priest who said mass gave a lovely homily. His pilgrimage was coming to an end too, and he spoke of his time in Medjugorje and how he would find it difficult to live the messages when he went home. He asked for prayers so he would be able to live Our Lady's messages and promised he'd pray for all of us. Sims and myself both turned and looked at one another through our watery eyes. We both fought hard to hold those tears in, a fight we both won - just..! I began to think about how Sean, Sims and myself had become very close in the past few days. It was going to be hard to say goodbye when they'd go back to the

U.S.A. I'll just have to go over and see them, I thought, this gave me some comfort.

After Holy Mass we made our way back to our house to await collection for our journey to the airport in Split. The journey was another opportunity to view the beautiful, Adriatic Sea. The coastline looked even more spectacular on the way back. Many of the local people were enjoying the summer sun, swimming and sunbathing. We passed many picturesque villages some bustling with people while others seemed quite peaceful. We stopped at a café halfway on our journey for refreshments. After a short break we boarded the buses and headed onwards on our journey. When we reached the airport we found that our flight was delayed and had to wait a number of hours. While in the airport Fr. Joe asked me if I could help him. He wanted to organise Holy Mass in Dublin the following morning and needed some things. He asked if I could telephone home and try and organise what he needed. So I called home for the first time since I left Dublin. When I was a child I had some minor problems with my hearing so I never liked using the telephone, as anyone who knows me well, will tell you. I had already told my Mam before leaving that I wouldn't phone home, so she was delighted to hear from me. This was a year or two before everyone started getting mobile phones. She asked me how I was getting on. I told her I had a great time and that I'd tell her later on. I asked her about getting stuff for Fr. Joe and told her that the flight was delayed. I then put Fr. Joe on to her and he told her exactly what he needed. Mam said she would organise it. Mam was now even more anxious and excited to hear how I got on. She said, "something wonderful must have happened, for Ken to have had a great time in Medjugorje". I was now bursting to tell her my experience after hearing her delight at my news. The plane eventually took off after the delay and we touched down in Dublin at about 10 o'clock at night. Mam, Dad and Gary were waiting in the airport for me. I introduced them to Sean and Sims; they were going on to a hotel with the group while I went home. They were departing for the U.S. the following morning after Holy Mass. In the car on the way home I told Mam and Dad all about my week and what had happened to me. Gary could not believe it; his ally was now on the other side. He remained very quiet in the back of the car. On our way home we called into my aunt Rita who was going through chemotherapy for Breast Cancer. She was one of the reasons I did not cancel the pilgrimage when the opportunity arose. I was now on such a high. I then told them all about my week and the apparition with Ivan. I gave her the wooden rosary beads I had when I was present at the apparition. I told her to give them back to me when she was finished all her treatment. She promised to take care of them. Months later she returned them when her treatment had finished. She still attends the hospital for check-ups and goes back every six months. Her doctor is very happy with her progress. She has had many little miracles with those rosary beads and Our Lady kept Rita in her mantle throughout her treatment and continues to look after her today. In May 1999 Rita came to Medjugorje in thanksgiving, more about that trip later. That first night home from Medjugorje I found it hard to sleep, I was on such an emotional high. I felt so happy for the time I had in Medjugorje.

The morning of Wednesday July 30, 1997, Mam, Dad and Myself went into the Dublin hotel to meet the American group for Holy Mass before they left for the airport. Fr. Joe was so grateful for items he requested for mass. We celebrated mass in a small hotel conference room. Afterwards, those departing boarded their bus to take them to the airport. I decided to travel to the airport with them and boarded the bus. Mam and Dad followed in the car. I sat with Sims and we chatted before we had to say our final goodbye in the airport. I gave Sean and Sims two cassettes each of my Dads albums as a parting gift. It was very hard saying goodbye to them; I promised I would visit them in the 'fall' as they say. They both lived in the Boston area. When they left, my pilgrimage was over and my new friends had another few hours left on theirs. But as I would learn later, this was only the beginning of my pilgrimage. I had to change and learn to love God with all my heart.

Note:
A lot happened in one week for me to remember. The following happened one of the mornings after Friday but the actual day is not important. We went to see Vicka, one of the visionaries. She stood on the steps of a house in Bijakovici at the base of apparition hill and gave a talk to the English speaking pilgrims. Simply seeing Vicka strengthened my newfound belief in God and the apparitions. I hope one day to have the joy and

happiness that she has. If the eyes are the windows to the soul like they say, Vicka's soul is clearly visible for all to see; it is bright, shiny and sparkles with love for God, Jesus and Our Blessed Mother. Someone later told me that Vicka physically suffers much and manages to speak to pilgrims most days, even when she is very sick. I felt a strong connection with her when I heard this, simply because of my CF. When her talk was over she came down to the bottom of the stairs from were she spoke. I was very close to her now. She reached out her hand and placed it on my head and prayed over me. An experience I will never forget. I could feel the pressure of her hand on my head for hours after the blessing. It was a very strange feeling. Our visit with Vicka had a big impact on me while in Medjugorje. Her joy is beautiful. Pray, pray, pray was the reoccurring message I remember about my week. Something I still try to do each day, but I am weak and fail to do this many many times. All these years later and I still struggle with my daily prayer life.

The following is the message given to the world by Our Lady on the evening of July 25th, 1997, the day my life changed. It seemed to say exactly what Fr. Joe had spoken about at the Blue Cross earlier that day.

MESSAGE OF 25th JULY 1997
"Dear Children! Today I invite you to respond to my call to prayer. I desire, dear children, that during this time you find a corner for personal prayer. I desire to lead you towards prayer with the heart. Only in this way will you comprehend that your life is empty without prayer. You will discover the meaning of your life when

you discover God in prayer. That is why, little children, open the door of your heart and you will comprehend that prayer is joy without which you cannot live. Thank you for having responded to my call."

Chapter 8

Re-adjusting at Home

Back home I found it hard for the first few days, weeks even. I was missing Medjugorje. I was not use to hearing the television, radio, telephone and even the doorbell of my house. These where all sounds I had not missed and forgotten about very quickly while in Medjugorje. Now I found I wanted to be away from these sounds and be silent. I tried to pray and found it hard. In Medjugorje it was easy to pray. I was thinking about Medjugorje often, and on many occasions I'd look at my watch and think "Oh - what would I be doing if I where in Medjugorje now". Not realising that I could be doing the exact same thing here. But I'd learn this later.

Some days on the bus going down to my granny's, I'd look at other passengers and think to myself, "I wonder if they know God?" If they did know God, well and good. If they didn't know God, it made me wonder, "why not?" I seemed to be thinking about God all the time. But that was all I was doing: thinking, not praying. Slowly I began to fall back into old habits and soon I was watching too much television and doing most of the things I was doing before I went to Medjugorje. However, I was now going to mass on Sundays again. I tried to pray everyday, but old habits still seemed to rule my head and heart. Days would pass at times before I'd say sorry to God for forgetting to acknowledge him. I still pray for the grace to be able to pray everyday.

After Medjugorje I was motivated to learn about God and my relationship with him. After a few weeks I wanted to get involved with something in my parish, but I didn't know what. I then decided I would look for something when I got back from my arranged trip to America in October. I didn't want to commit myself to something and then say, "oh, I'm going to America for a few weeks, sorry about that". So I waited until after my trip. In America I stayed with Mattie and Mary in Boston. They were delighted to see me after my pilgrimage. I told them all about my trip and they listened with joy as I related story after story. They thanked God for my experience and joked with me, "finally, she (Our Lady) got you".

While in Boston Fr. Joe had a Medjugorje reunion mass in his parish, where I met up with all my new friends. It was great to see Sean, Sims and catch up with each other. The trip passed very quickly and all too soon it was time for me to return home. On the plane, I wondered when I'd see my friends again and what I could get involved in when I got home. Little did I know, but Our Lady had sorted it all out and it was already waiting for me.

Chapter 9

Prayer Group

When I arrived in Dublin airport Mam, Lorna and Gary were waiting for me. In the car on the way home Mam told me that, Ed who was in Medjugorje with me was looking for me the previous day. Mam had told him I was away but I'd be home the following day.

Later that day Philip and Ed's mother, Patricia, called in. She told me that she had just returned from Medjugorje, and while there she was talking with a young couple, Aaron and Paula who were on their honeymoon, Aaron was a neighbour of hers. They told her of their plans to start a young adult prayer group when they returned home. They asked her if she knew any young people who might be interested. So she thought of me and said she would ask me. As she was telling me this I thought to myself, this was Our Lady working at high speed. The first meeting was planned for Wednesday and this was the Tuesday evening. Our Lady wastes no time, I thought to myself. I told Patricia that I was very interested and planned to meet Ed the following evening. The prayer meeting would be held in Aaron and Paula's House.

The following evening I met Ed and we walked to the local bus stop where we met Catherine, a friend of the Ed's family, who was doing the driving. Catherine had been to Medjugorje and was also interested in joining the prayer group. On the way over to Aaron and Paula's I was nervous about meeting them. I remembered Aaron as a kid but had not seen him in years. I didn't really know him. When we arrived, Aaron opened the front door and greeted us warmly. He then introduced us to Paula who welcomed us to their home. We all sat in their living room and just talked about Medjugorje. We all relaxed quickly and chatted for hours. I told them that on my way over in the car I was thinking, "what have I done, they might be religious freaks". Paula said she was thinking the same as the car pulled up outside their home. We all had a Laugh and agreed that we weren't as bad as we had feared. We all agreed to meet again the following week. We all said a decade of the rosary before we left as we felt Our Lady had definitely brought us together. No doubt what so ever.

Over the following weeks we met every Wednesday in Aaron and Paula's home. At first we had no real structure to the evening, but soon we began to work something out. After a few weeks things seemed to fall into place. We called the prayer group Corpus Christi. Each meeting seemed to bond us together; we shared so much and helped each other.

The weeks passed quickly and it was now coming up to advent and the prayer group was going strong with a new member since our first meeting, Marie. Marie worked with Aaron and came along after Aaron told her about Medjugorje and the prayer group. Marie had not yet been to Medjugorje. Philip, Ed's brother was home from Medjugorje for the winter months. He joined the prayer group while at home and we all prepared for Christmas. On the final Sunday of advent we had our last prayer meeting of the year. We had others attend this meeting who'd been along to the group at one stage or another since it started. Mary, one of the Irish girls whom I went to the waterfall along with Sean and Sims while I was in Medjugorje came along too. She had met Aaron and Paula when they were on their honeymoon. We had a wonderful prayerful day and shared gifts and stories with each other. It was a very special way to prepare for Christmas.

Chapter 10

Eucharistic Adoration

One evening after one of our prayer meetings, Paula asked me why I didn't go to Adoration on Tuesdays in my local church. "Adoration, what's that" I thought to myself. "These people go to Adoration and I don't even know what it is." So I enquired about it and said I didn't know they had it in our church. I also reminded them that I was new to this religion thing, jokingly. We laughed and Paula said I should come along next week. I promised I would, not really knowing what Adoration was.

For those of you who don't know what Adoration is, here is an explanation. Adoration is when the priest takes a consecrated communion host and places it in a monstrance. (Monstrance comes from the Latin "monstrare" to show, expose and to view.) The monstrance is then placed in front of the tabernacle or on the altar of the church or chapel for adoration. The faithful pray before Jesus usually in silent prayer.

The following Tuesday I went along to Adoration from 9pm to 10pm. I found it the longest hour I'd ever spent in a church. An hour in silence was alien to me, not to mention a an hour in silent prayer. I found it very hard to pray and was distracted by the slightest noise. Afterwards, I went back to Aaron's parent's house for a cup of tea with Aaron and Paula. Aaron's parent's have both been to Medjugorje and are very warm hearted and friendly. I told Aaron and Paula that I found the hour very long. They said that they felt the same the first time they went to Adoration. They said I would love it after a few weeks. I didn't believe them, but promised myself I'd give it a chance. I went along the following week and didn't find it much easier. Thankfully and slowly I began to enjoy the peace and quiet prayer. Each week seemed to get easier and soon I loved going. Adoration was my time to get back in touch with God. As I said earlier, some days I'd forget to bless myself, let alone pray.

In Adoration I found I had time to talk and pray with God, but more importantly be still and let God speak to my heart. Some weeks, I would just stare at the monstrance with the flickering candles in the darkness. Barely praying at all. It made me feel close to God, it was very cosy at times, especially when I'd been having a hard week. The stillness of the church was homely, so relaxing and at times the hour passed too quickly. Every Tuesday there were only a handful of people in the church for Adoration, but I always imagined the church to be full with angels and saints.

Be still and know that I am God.

Chapter 11

Three Weeks in the Valley

As I write this, I must explain that since Medjugorje to this point of my journey I was getting the message of Medjugorje wrong. God knew it, Jesus knew it and Our Lady knew it, but I didn't, I hadn't a clue. Our Lady and God however, were busy with the remedy that would hopefully get the correct message to me once and for all.

In the New Year we as a prayer group planned to go to Medjugorje in June for two weeks. When the arrangements were being made, my Mam and Dad were planning to go to Medjugorje in June too. But they were due to fly out the day I would be retuning home, so I decided to stay for another week. This meant I would be spending a total of three weeks in Medjugorje.

In the months leading up to our pilgrimage we continued with the prayer meeting every week. We all became very close and shared so much with each other. Our Lady brought us all together to help each other and teach us to pray more. Some weeks I found it hard to pray and the prayer meeting would get me back on track and in touch with God. As the weeks passed the date of our departure to Medjugorje grew closer. Everyone in the group became more excited about our pilgrimage.

Then the day came for my second trip to Medjugorje, June 2nd, 1998. The flight to Spilt was fine. On the bus to Medjugorje I had a great sense of something that

Aaron had said at one of our prayer meetings. He said the second time he went to Medjugorje was like he was going home. I began to understand what he meant. I also had the feeling one has as a child when going on holiday, it seemed like such a long journey because the longing was so great. I was bursting with excitement at the thoughts of reaching our destination. I enjoyed the bus ride; we all sat together down the back. The bus had a table that we all sat around. We travelled in style until we went around sharp bends, of which there are many on the way to Medjugorje. So we slid all over place. We arrived in Medjugorje at around 10.30pm and were staying in a lovely house down a lane way behind the house I stayed in the previous year. After supper I went down to see the church with Aaron, Paula and Marie. When we reached the church it was midnight and the birds sang once again. I could sense the peace as I prayed before the statue of Our Lady on the church grounds. As I walked back to our house with Aaron, we both felt that this pilgrimage was going to be special for us all and for the prayer group. It was a lovely warm evening.

The following morning we got up for Holy Mass. Before entering mass I became aware of some people looking at the sun, which was rising above Apparition Hill. I turned to my left and noticed a rainbow that was shaped like a tied ribbon. It surrounded the sun. I had read and heard of many signs and wonders in Medjugorje, but to witness this was amazing. Once more I felt that this was going to a very special pilgrimage.

At the opening meeting after mass I was amazed at the number of first time pilgrims. Later that night I went to Adoration. It was held out in the open at the back of the church. Over the past six months I had grown to love Adoration. Attending adoration in Medjugorje is very special. One gets a real sense of universal communion with God, as there are so many people from all over the world praying and adoring Jesus at the same time. Father Slavko, led the prayers during the holy hour. Beautifully simple hymns were sung in many languages. One gets a great sense of unity and love for God. It was an amazing experience one that I will never forget. The peace I felt is something that I cannot describe in words.

On Thursday morning Aaron and Paula announced they were expecting a baby. I was delighted to hear this wonderful news. The week seemed to be getting better by the minute. On Friday however, I woke up with strange feelings, I started to doubt why I was back in Medjugorje and spiritually I was not feeling as I did when I left Medjugorje the previous year. I began to think that there was something wrong with me because of these feelings. It was early on in the pilgrimage and I had these negative feelings. That afternoon I was by myself praying at the then new 'Statue of the Risen Lord', behind the church. I was wondering if I would feel the same joy and peace as before. I was afraid because I was here for the next three weeks and if I didn't feel the same it may be a big disappointment. So when things get though, what do I do best? Yes - I challenged Our Lady and God. I was sitting in the shadow of the statue, because the sun was extremely hot, it was near 3pm and no one else was around. I was sitting looking down at the pebbles that formed the pathway that led to and surround the statue. I said to Our Lady, "Let me find a cross-shaped stone" as I brushed my hand across the pebbles in front of me. I didn't find any cross-shaped stone and thought, "what am I doing." I said to myself, "Ken, just be happy you're here" and I forgot about the cross shaped stone.

On Saturday morning we were going to make our way up Mt. Krizivac, Cross Mountain. The morning was nice and fresh. We had an early start to the day, 5am in the morning early because of the heat wave Medjugorje was experiencing. I decided to be careful and not rush the climb. The Stations of the Cross lead pilgrims to the top of the mountain and are spaced out every few hundred yards. I took my time and rested at each station. I was delighted to make it to the top and enjoyed the incredible views. The previous year I had no desire to make it to the top, when I could have done so. This time it was different, I wanted to make it to the top. While there, I prayed beneath the big white cross for a while and thanked God for this wonderful pilgrimage and the friends I had made since my first visit to Medjugorje. I then went and found a quiet spot so I could listen to my personal stereo. I was listening to my song "Far Away". I had written and sung it on my Dad's latest album. The song is about my conversion in Medjugorje. I also prayed for all my family, friends and my special American friends that I made in Medjugorje last year, especially for Sean and Sims. I had told them of my plans for a three-week pilgrimage when I saw them in America in March earlier in the year. After about thirty minutes on top of Mt. Krizivac I started my decent so I would be down in time for Holy Mass.

Later that day, I went down to the church for the evening program. It is so relaxing to sit outside listening and participating in the rosary and Croatian mass. I especially liked sitting on the benches in front of the confessionals, watching the birds that had their nests on the church roof and towers. They seem to be as happy as anybody else to be in Medjugorje, it's fascinating to watch them swoop down and chase each other while they constantly chirp and sing. (I have to say that I miss them, their nests are no longer on the church, and the trees are long since gone too). That night Adoration was held on the outside altar. The young men from the Cenacolo community 'Campo Della Vita' sung the adoration hymns and played the music. They are a great example of what God can do in one's life. Some of the happiest people I saw in Medjugorje on my first trip were in the Cenacolo community, totally changed from their previous lifestyle. They are a real inspiration to me. Once again Fr. Slavko led the prayers at Adoration; 'I could listen to his voice all night'.

This year when we went to the Cenacolo community we heard two testimonies, one of the boys gave the answer to a question "what do we get from adoration?" He said that some of the boys do not like praying in adoration when they first enter community. Praying is something alien to these boys and to the life they'd been living. As a community they have to pray, work and eat together. He said some of the boys get bored while praying and don't understand what is happening. But slowly they learn to love adoration, not really knowing why. He then compared it to workmen who work outdoors in the summer months. He said, they get a suntan without wanting or realising they are doing so, not until later. He said adoration is the same, the boys do not realise they receive many graces, not until later. I will never forget his answer. It made me realise how important adoration is. Especially at times when I don't feel it is doing me any good. But spending time in Adoration will always do us good.

On the Sunday everyone in our house met at the candle area beside the church to pray. It was a lovely evening of prayer and singing, I brought my guitar and we sang between the different prayers. I prayed for Mr. Henry (Grandad), who was very sick in Boston and for all the Henry family, plus everyone else I could think of.

The next day Fr. Slavko gave a talk on Our Lady's messages. The meeting was held in the dome at the back of the church. He went through Our Lady's latest monthly message given on May 25, 1998; Fr. Slavko explained it so beautifully and made everything practical and easy to understand. I have to say it was the first time I experienced God the Fathers love for me. Some of the things Fr. Slavko said made me realise what I had missed the previous year while in Medjugorje. On that occasion I felt Mary's motherly love, and I found myself praying more to her since. I suddenly realised in that moment why Our Lady had brought me back for three weeks. Our Lady invited me back for her to say, "Ken I love you so much, but you have missed the point. God's is your creator and He's the One to pray too. I will help you pray and I will pray for you, all you have to do is ask." I'd now realised the mistake I had made and that Our Lady had indeed given me a cross-shaped stone, but not in the place I had wanted it. She led me up Cross Mountain and gave me what I asked for; the biggest cross-shaped stone for miles around. I could almost hear her clapping her hands slowly and saying, "finally he gets it, I led you to Adoration, but you kept praying to me, my child what more must I do." I laughed at how I had missed the signs that Our Lady had put before me. I missed them all and I nearly missed the Stone Cross too.

That same day, during dinner Philip came with the itinerary for the following day. Afterwards he said he wanted a word with me outside. When I went out, Philip told me that Mr. Henry in Boston had died the previous day. He told me Mr. Henry died very peacefully. I was very sad to hear this news. I was so glad that I had prayed for 'Grandad' the night before at the prayer meeting. It was a great comfort for me knowing that 'Grandad' was only a few hours from Delia and Noel when I offered up those prayers for him and all the Henry family. I got upset when I returned to the dinner table. Everyone was great to me, especially Marie. She came outside to me after dinner and we had a good chat.

Later Michael, our group leader and neighbour of mine, had planned for our group to go the Blue Cross after Our Lady's Apparition that evening. I was delighted to go because the Blue Cross means so much to all the Henry family. I went and prayed for Mattie, Mary, Winnie, Tommy and Lori and all the grandchildren especially Marty and Erin. The next few weeks were going to be horrible for the whole family. 'Grandad' was such a great man of faith who loved Our Lady so much. I can still see and hear him laughing; he had a great laugh. Memories are a great consolation. Rest in Peace 'Grandad'.

Monday morning at breakfast I noticed that a lot of people from our house had big smiles on their faces. Our Lady and God had obviously revealed their love to them in whatever way they seemed fitting. After all, they do know all our ambitions, hopes, desires, dreams and fears. They know us better than we know ourselves.

On Tuesday, the rest of the group's final morning, I woke early and decided to write Mattie and Mary a letter so I could send it home and get it posted to America. I hoped it would be a comfort for them to have someone pray for them in Medjugorje at this time, because it's the closest place to heaven on earth. After Holy Mass we went to the church's car park to see our fellow pilgrims off. A few minutes before the buses departed for the airport, a lady got off one of the buses and ran over to me. She told me that I reminded her of her nephew in England. She then handed me a laminated card (about the size of a credit card) with her prayer group's name written on it. She said, "That's for you". I looked at her and she was smiling at me, as if to say "isn't it great". I turned the card over to see what was on the other side. As I did so, she said, "I felt I should give you that". I looked at the card which had one word printed in a large font on the back. The word 'JESUS' printed in bold capital letters. It was great..!!!

Suddenly the message Our Lady had been telling me all week, was on a laminated card for me to take home. I was a little slow in getting Our Lady's message but now I had no excuse. I carry that card in my wallet all the time, so I never forget what and who's the most important person in my life.

Later that day it began to rain. We couldn't believe it. After a week of well over thirty degree temperatures the rain was so refreshing, it was lovely. The raindrops were those big heavy drops that hurt as they bounced off your head. Even the bells in the church rang in thanksgiving. The local farmers must have been delighted to see some rain. The rain only lasted about forty-five minutes. After the evening program we went up Podbrdo for an Apparition with Ivan and his prayer group. There were hundreds of people up on the hill when we arrived. The prayer group, were singing hymns in several languages, it was lovely. We found a place close to the Cross and prayed in anticipation of Our Lady's apparition with Ivan. When we got back to the house later that night a new group of pilgrims had arrived and gone to bed after their journey.

Week 2: A Journey with Fr. Svet (Svetozar)

The second week began with Catherine from our prayer group arriving to join us. At Holy Mass I saw Fr. Pat Butler, a family friend on the Altar. He was with a group from Waterford in the southeast of Ireland. He noticed me and smiled. After mass I introduced him to our small group. He gave me a copy of an article he'd asked me to write for a new magazine in his area. It was about my experience on my first pilgrimage to Medjugorje. That afternoon at three O'clock Fr. Svet from the parish was giving a talk in the dome. After his talk I went up to him and introduced myself to him. Fr. Svet knows my parents and was delighted to see me and gave me a big hug. I then introduced him to Aaron, Marie and Catherine. Paula had gone back to the house as she was not feeling well and the heat was not helping her. Fr. Svet wanted to meet us after Mass the next day to go somewhere with him to have a chat. He was so happy to see us. Everyone was delighted I went over to him because the following day was the feast of Corpus Christi, the name of our prayer group. Yet again God's master plan was working well. As always..!!!

The following day, Fr. Svet celebrated Holy Mass in St. James' Church. His homily was about seeking the Body of Christ in everyone that we meet. His word were inspiring and made me think hard about myself. After Mass we met Fr. Svet outside the church. He was not ready to meet us and asked us to come back at 1:30pm. We went to Colombo restaurant and got something to eat and drink. When we finished we walked over to the rectory. As we got there Fr. Svet came out of the rectory door with Fr. Slavko. They both chatted as they came down the steps; Fr. Slavko walked towards the church while Fr. Svet began walking towards his car and beckoned us to follow. We all piled into his little car, Paula in the front, as she was looking after two, "The Baby" as Fr. Svet reminded us. On leaving the church grounds Fr. Svet told us we were going to visit Mostar. He then became our tour guide as we left Medjugorje, pointing out vineyards and many things of interest. We said three Our Father's: Hail Mary's and Glory Be's for a safe journey.

The journey was eye opening. We passed many houses that where either destroyed or abandoned during the recent Balkan war. Hundreds of empty houses that once had people and families living in them are now a part of history and left to decay. I hope and pray those families are not forgotten whether they are dead or alive. Seeing images of this war on television was easy to watch and even easier to forget. To actually pass these images for real brings home how terrible War is. Now the war was made real in my mind, it became personal, not just something I'd seen on television.

When we got to Mostar, Fr. Svet brought us to the new cathedral that the Franciscans were building. The old cathedral was destroyed during the war. When we walked in the massive entrance (no doors were erected at that time) all the scaffolding was standing empty. As it was a feast day all the workers had a day off. No interior work had started yet, mostly structural work. Fr. Svet lead us up to the choir loft. The whole cathedral is going hold a few thousand people when its finished. We then made our way back down the steps. Fr. Svet began talking to two nuns who were sweeping and washing the floor. Fr. Svet told us that there was a big celebration tonight and to follow him. He made his way down the steps with one of the nuns. We went down and found ourselves on a balcony looking down on a room with hundreds of chairs laid out, ready for Holy Mass. Fr. Svet told us that they were for that night's celebration. It was such a beautiful sight. Behind the altar was the Divine Mercy icon, to the left of the altar was a statue of Our Lady and the Infant Child; to the right was statue of Jesus on the cross. Lights were brought in for the mass, as the church hadn't any fitted.

We could not believe the sight. It was like we had uncovered a secret church. We were like children on Christmas morning after discovering Santa Claus had visited. We were so surprised to see it because of all the building work going on upstairs. We stayed there for a few minutes to pray, absorb the atmosphere and take it all in. We then went to the old monastery that is attached to the new cathedral. Walking the corridors we began to notice the bullet holes in some of the steps, doors and walls. I thought about the turmoil this place has been through, it's heartbreaking and very thought provoking. We then came across a prayer garden in the courtyard. Just as we did there was another downpour of rain. Fr. Svet led us up more stairs until we reached a tiny lift. This lift was built for about three people but the six of us squashed in. Paula said that she didn't like it one bit. When we all spilled out of the lift Fr. Svet brought us up another two flight of stairs and into an artist's workshop. The artist was still making wooden Stations of the Cross for the Cathedral. The plaques that he had finished were beautiful. Fr. Svet showed us his favourite, the sixth station, when Veronica wipes the face of Jesus. The detail in all the Stations were incredible, but this one was particularly beautiful. Then Fr. Svet said that he came to see something else but he didn't know where it was. Time to move on.

We left the workshop and followed Fr. Svet, he started opening all these doors and peeping in. After looking through a number of doors he said, "Ah, it's here" and he entered. We followed again. One by one we got to the door. A huge stained glass window was laid out on the floor of this room. It was Fr. Svet's first time to see the window and its beauty amazed him. The design was of the Nativity and was made of different coloured and textured glass. The window was made in sections that slotted together like a jigsaw puzzle. The artist was the same one who was making the Stations of the Cross we'd seen earlier. We then walked down to the side chapel of the cathedral where the stained glass window was to be placed when finished. Fr. Svet told us the next time we'd see the window it would be in the cathedral. After our tour of the cathedral we walked over to a nearby apartment block.

Fr. Svet told us his niece lived on the fifth floor and we should call to see her. From the outside the apartments looked very rundown. I couldn't believe people still lived in them. They were also badly damaged during the war. He then told us the lifts were broken and we'd have to use the stairs. The complex was in darkness except for the small amount of sunlight that found its way in. We made our way up the stairs. When we got to his niece's flat there was no answer when he knocked. Fr. Svet then decided to call to a couple and their son that he knew, they lived on the ninth floor. Their son opened the door and inside an elderly couple made us feel very welcome. The woman was unable to leave the flat because she was confined to a wheelchair and because the lift was broken. She hadn't been outside in a number of years. She said the next time she leaves would be in a box. We were surprised to hear this as she said it with a big smile. We were offered drinks and stayed about twenty minutes before making our way back down the stairs.

Driving back to Medjugorje we passed a graveyard in Mostar. Fr. Svet told us it used to be a public park. Later in the journey we were all very quiet contemplating what we had seen. Fr. Svet, after a few minutes noticed this and asked us what we were thinking. We all mumbled something, but nothing that made much sense. Fr. Svet pointed out that we'd seen many things, but no sad or unhappy people. Though their situations were difficult, he asked if we knew why? We were not sure how to answer. Then Fr. Svet said, "Because they have God." The atmosphere changed immediately. He was right; we hadn't seen any unhappy people.

As we chatted, one of the topics that came up in conversation was, why do people go on Pilgrimage? Marie asked all kinds of questions and told Fr. Svet how she was getting on so far on her pilgrimage. She spoke of all the worries she had about coming on pilgrimage. Also the fear she had if she did not feel anything in Medjugorje. Fr. Svet said it's a question he hears all the time. He said the only reason we should go on pilgrimage is for God. One does not have to feel anything on pilgrimage he said. Once we make the effort to make a pilgrimage, that is enough. If we look at it in this way the pilgrimage will not be a disappointment, because we do it for God. You can't disappoint God by going on pilgrimage. The rest of the journey back to Medjugorje passed really quickly. We thanked Fr. Svet for his time and a wonderful day.

After evening mass there was a Eucharistic procession around the church and part of the village for Corpus Christi feast day celebrations. All the local people were out including children dressed in their communion clothes. They threw rose petals before the procession. It was lovely to see and it topped of a wonderful day in Medjugorje and Mostar.

The next few days the prayer group grew closer and shared a lot with each other. We experienced wonders as a group and individually, like the sun spinning, which we all read about and never thought we'd see. One other magical wonder that stands out in my mind is a sight I had never seen before and haven't seen anything like it since. One night we were walking down the lane way that lead to our house. It was a lovely night with a full moon and the odd cloud here and there in the starry sky. As we walked I looked upward and noticed a cloud drift past the moon. I saw there were moon rays, just like sun rays breaking through clouds on an overcast day. But these moon rays silhouetted the cloud; this cloud literally had a silver lining. It was a beautiful sight. I have never noticed it before at home, and I haven't seen it since so it remains a special experience to me.

All too soon the end of the second week in Medjugorje was upon us, and time to say goodbye to my friends. The previous two weeks had been a true blessing for the prayer group. I decided to travel with them to Split airport and say goodbye and also welcome my family and friends (My, parents, Gary, my Nana Vera (Dad's Mother), Carla (my Cousin), Betty (my aunt), Hugh (my uncle) and Susan (our Neighbour)).

On the bus to the airport we had a great time. We had a singsong session with Fr. Pat and his group from Waterford whom we also spent some time with during the week. Fr. Pat is a great family friend. When we got to the airport the inbound flight was delayed for hours. We spent these hours talking in the airport restaurant and watching the arrival display screen for any change in the arrival time. After several changes in time we watched and cheered as the plane touched down. Everyone then went through the departure gate. I said goodbye to Aaron, Paula, Marie, Catherine, Ed and Fr. Pat. I then met my family; they barely recognised me as I had a great suntan from all the sunshine. It was late when the buses left Split for Medjugorje. We arrived in Medjugorje at about 5.30 in the morning; everyone was very tired and went straight to bed. It was good to see my family.

Week 3: The Family

My third week was a great week for all my family members who'd come out. They all had a great week and all found their pilgrimage a wonderful experience and fell in love with Medjugorje, although some won't admit it publicly.!!! This final week seemed to pass by really quickly, and soon I had to think about going home. I knew I'd miss Medjugorje but felt happy leaving, I told myself I'd be back next year, that made leaving Medjugorje easier.

I was glad in another way to be going home having spent three weeks in Medjugorje. Towards the end of my pilgrimage I was looking forward to seeing the rest of my family and friends. But like I said, it's hard to leave Medjugorje. The peace I feel when I'm there is hard to explain. It's like; a child who knows that mother is close by and feels safe and secure. The child is happy and content knowing that their mother is close by, in case the child needs her. I feel so peaceful and close to Heaven when I pray in Medjugorje. Alarm bells might be going off in your head now as you read this – "Hello...!!! Who's this Nut", "Close to Heaven", "aah come on, get a grip Ken". I know exactly how you feel; I felt the same way for a many years. No I didn't, I was much worse. Just ask anyone who knew me before I went to Medjugorje. It may sound very strange to some people, especially those who do not believe in God or those who are just skeptical about Medjugorje. Some might say "you don't need Medjugorje to feel like this". They are correct and God Bless them for having such great faith, but I didn't, not at that point of my journey anyway. I would have to learn about faith for myself. Today, I'm still trying to nurture my faith. Many times I loose sight of God. That's when I remember my experience in Medjugorje and I thank God and apologise to him. God knew exactly what it would take to make me believe and He used all His know how to get me to Medjugorje. The old me would have run a mile if I thought I would find God in Medjugorje, but God knew that, and He got me in His time using His

Mother, very clever. Thank God, for His ways are not ours.

All that I can say to people that find the apparitions in Medjugorje difficult to believe in because they have lasted so long, is don't judge Medjugorje until they have visited. As Fr. Slavko has said on many occasions, "Come and See". I judged and ridiculed Medjugorje for years until I discovered that I was wrong when I experienced it for myself.

In Medjugorje I changed my thinking after I opened my heart to the possibility that God existed. In this tiny village miles from my home I'd arrived with so much hurt that I had hardened my heart and had denied Gods existence and the happenings in Medjugorje. However, God knew all my thoughts, my feelings and wasted no time in showing me that 'I was indeed wrong' and loved. He showed me that He existed and the apparitions of Our Blessed Lady in Medjugorje are true. My hard heart had melted and was now like putty in God's hands. God had plans for me and immediately began to mould me into a better person . I had thought that I was happy until the moment God showed me a NEW happiness, he revealed His unconditional Love for me. He loves each and everyone of us equally and very personally.

While in Medjugorje I realised that I was an atheist who deep down, believed in God but wouldn't admit it to anyone before. I suspect most atheists are believers deep in their heart. So deep, that most don't know it yet. I feared going to Medjugorje for years, I feared I might rediscover God. I didn't want to be seen as someone weak who needed a God. I thought I was strong enough on my own, and that only weak people believed in God. But now after my experience in Medjugorje I don't care what people think of me, I know in my heart that God exists and I pray for those who don't know of His Love yet!

Chapter 12

My Surprise Trip Back to Medjugorje

I got home to Dublin on the June 23, two days before the 17th anniversary of the apparitions. Medjugorje was really crowded when we left and the weather was getting hotter. Last July in Medjugorje the weather was too hot for me and I lost too much weight walking around in the heat. For me this is bad because I can't afford to lose weight. I find it so hard to put on weight, I have to take supplement drinks to try and get extra calories. A lot of people with CF have poor appetites because of the nature of the illness, and I'm no exception. One doctor told me that my brain is so busy concentrating on breathing that it doesn't tell my body that I'm hungry and that I should be eating. So leaving Medjugorje with its rising temperatures was made that bit easier for this reason.

However, having spent three weeks in Medjugorje I found it very hard to settle back home. I found myself contemplating my life and what I should do with myself. I felt I was a lot quieter; I didn't know why I was feeling this way and was worried that these feelings would not go away. God knew my feelings and my worries. Our Lady had me in her mantle also. A few weeks after returning home from their first trip, Carla and Susan decided they wanted to go back to Medjugorje in August. They asked if I would go with them. I had not planned on going back so soon, but how could I refuse? I told myself, Our Lady must want me back for a reason.

We'd arranged to go back for the last week of August. We touched down in Split in golden sunshine once again. We met our guide Claudia in the airport who was surprised to see us back so soon. On arrival in Medjugorje we were shown our house, it was the house I had stayed in early June. Our host family could not believe that I was back in Medjugorje so soon either. They welcomed me with hugs and big smiles. There were about twenty others staying in the house, all strangers as we began our pilgrimage together.

That first night back in Medjugorje I began questioning why I was back so soon. I was tired after a long day of traveling. Then Fr. Svet's words of wisdom came back to my mind as I pondered, "Say your pilgrimage is for God". So, I put his words into practice and remembered that special day when we travelled back from Mostar earlier in the summer. I thanked God for Fr. Svet and left the pilgrimage in God's hands.

The next morning I woke up feeling refreshed and excited about the rest of the week. At breakfast the group were very quiet. Nobody really knew anyone so they just ate breakfast and left for Holy Mass. It's Strange looking at people's faces on the first morning of a pilgrimage; some people look terrified, some sad and others apprehensive. I suppose I looked terrified the first time I was in Medjugorje. Others were happy and cheerful, this made it easy to tell that they'd been to Medjugorje before, I presumed. As the week went on the atmosphere in the house became very friendly as everyone got to know one another and God. Carla, Sue and myself became very good friends with Regina, Louise and John from County Galway, in Ireland. Louise and John were just married and Regina is Louise's sister. We had noticed them looking at us early in the week, in Colombo restaurant. We'd recognised them from our house and wondered if they were okay or religious freaks! Me judging again, I really need to change my ways. Subsequently they thought the same about us and we all had a good laugh about our first impressions. Regina and Louise had been to Medjugorje before, while it was John's first time.

We shared a lot with each other as the week progressed and had a great week. We all had our own personal experiences with God and Our Blessed Lady, all of which strengthened our faith. The week passed with some beautiful memories and some hilariously funny moments, which brought us closer to God and to our new friends. We were even interviewed for an Irish Newspaper, on why we came to Medjugorje. As we were young, and in the age of technology and any other "dot com" one can think of, the reporter, figured we must be fanatics or brainwashed to go on pilgrimage. I think we convinced the reporter that we were normal young people and not fanatics. We were on pilgrimage because we believed in God and wanted to deepen our faith. He seemed to think it odd that people need to go on pilgrimage in today's world. Why do you need to go on pilgrimage? I could only tell him how I felt. I told him that I found Medjugorje very peaceful. "Why can't you have the same peace at home?" he asked. I told him if I had the same feeling of peace at home as I do when I'm here I'd be happy never to come Medjugorje again.

But, "until the day I receive that grace I will come back to Medjugorje as often as I can", I told him. As Carmel, a friend and neighbour says, "It recharges the batteries until next year". This pilgrimage was a true gift from God with many blessings.

Once again, and all too quickly the week was over and we were saying goodbye in Dublin Airport to our new friends. People who've been to Medjugorje a number of times say that it is a different experience every time and in most cases better. This seems to be true for me too. I'm slowly beginning to realise that you don't have to be in Medjugorje to feel the Joy and Peace that one finds in Medjugorje. One has to pray everyday to keep in touch with God. I still find this hard and continue to learn how to pray everyday. I still make excuses when I don't pray, when deep down I know I should be praying more and more.In an ever-changing world, distractions are everywhere. Laziness towards prayer is a struggle for me. I want to love God more, I've been reading books and listening to audiocassettes and CD's about Medjugorje, to try and inspire me and bring me closer to God. I'm interested in how God and Our Lady have changed the lives of so many people in and through Medjugorje. These stories inspire me to love God and I try to see Jesus in everyone I meet. It's hard!

Of the materials that I've read or listened too, Our Lady and God have brought most of the authors and makers of these into my life, either before or after I'd been to Medjugorje, people like Tom Rutkoski (Gospa Missions), Michael O'Brien, Sister Emmanuel, Wayne Wieble, Heather Parsons and Fr. Svetozar and many more. I've met some of these people while in America at a Marion Conference that Dad was giving his testimony at in 1994. At the time I thought most of the people at this conference were mad. Our Lady was leading me gently on my journey to God, so gently that I was unaware of it, even when God was all around me . One thing I did notice about that trip to America in 1994 was at how hard Dad works when he goes to these events. We thought he got to see these places when he'd travel all over America, but in most cases he would only see the hotel rooms, the venue he'd be witnessing at and then the journey by car or plane to the next destination. So it was all work, hardly any play and no sight seeing. So we got to understand just what he was going through on most of his trips to America and around the world. Exhausting work, as we found out. America is such a vast country.

Chapter 13

A New Direction

Since my trip to Medjugorje in June 98, my health began to get slightly worse. At the start of my three weeks in Medjugorje of that June I was on my 'backup' medication, for I a chest infection. This backup combined with my normal maintenance of daily medications, vitamins and nebulizers helped my infection and I felt good in Medjugorje. Whenever these backup medications failed to fight any infection it would mean that I would need a hospital admission for IV antibiotics.

After my trip in August '98, I got another chest infection and had to go on my backup again. This worked and I was ok for another few months until the beginning of November when, Susan and myself went to Galway for a weekend to see Regina, Louise and John. Louise was in hospital and scheduled for discharge while we were there. I had a chest infection and was on my backup once again. As you can see a pattern was starting to emerge. However it didn't stop us having a great weekend, catching up and showing each other our photographs of our pilgrimage to Medjugorje. On Sunday evening we said goodbye to Regina and her lovely family, who kindly put us up for the weekend.

After our weekend away it was now the middle of November and Christmas was fast approaching. The prayer group continued to meet every Wednesday.

Carla and Susan joined us whenever they could. We had our last prayer meeting the Wednesday before Christmas and broke up the prayer group until further notice. Paula and Aaron were due to have their baby at the end of January. So we did not want to impose on them in the final weeks of their pregnancy.

The week before Christmas I was feeling very sick and went on my backup medication again. It got me through the festive season, but when I finished the backup I felt lousy again. On New Year's Eve, I spent the New Year countdown on my own. Everyone was out at different New Years parties, I wanted them all to go out and enjoy themselves; I was just happy that I didn't have to go out anywhere.

Early in January 1999 Dad was going to America for a double hip replacement. He needed them both replaced because his pain was becoming unbearable. Years of taking steroids for his Crohns disease had damaged his hip joints. I was still feeling miserable as Dad flew to Jackson Hole, Wyoming on January 5th, for his surgery. His surgery went very well but another problem arose from the anesthetic. His bowel shut down, his bowel had been weakened because of all his previous bowel surgeries. He was very ill as a result.

Meanwhile, I was really feeling terrible, but said nothing. I didn't want to worry Mam any further. However after about ten days when I knew Dad was getting better, I decided to tell my Mam how lousy I felt. We decided to go to hospital. When I got in the car I became very upset because I knew I'd have to stay in hospital. Mam said something that made me think as we pulled out of the driveway, she said, "maybe God wants you there to help others." I was upset because I hadn't had a hospital admission since September 1994, some four and half years previously. As we got closer to the hospital I knew that I needed IV's, I felt so sick and miserable. I was admitted through the accident and emergency department. I decided Mam was right; maybe God did want me in hospital for whatever reason. I just had to be aware of it. I was in hospital two days when I got a phone call from Aaron to say Paula had given birth to a healthy baby girl, Naomi, this was very good news.

After a few days of tests, doctors discovered I had pneumonia and began treating me with IV's. They also discovered I had developed diabetes, as some people with CF do as the pancreas is affected by CF too. The diabetes is what had caused all the symptoms I was having at home, the tiredness, thirst, frequent passing of urine and high temps. They began treating the Diabetes with insulin injections before my main meals. They kept a close check on my blood sugar levels because I was on steroids; and they caused the levels to rise. After a few days I began to feel better and I was getting back to myself. I was glad they could tell me what was causing those unusual symptoms. The diabetic nurse taught me how to test my own blood sugar level and how to inject myself with insulin.

The usual length of treatment for my chest infections is a two-week coarse of IV antibiotics. However, after about a week of treatment Dr. Gallagher, my consultant came and told me that one of the IV drugs was not fighting the infection, as my system had become resistant to it. That drug was stopped and a new one added which meant another two weeks in hospital.

A few days later, my doctor told me during rounds that the pneumonia was not clearing up on my right lung. He wanted me to have a bronchoscopy. This is when they put a tiny camera down into your lungs, and see what's going on and take a biopsy if necessary. I decided to take any treatment offered to me, as the doctors knew best, or so I thought at this point. I was happy to have this done, because I wanted to get out of hospital quickly.

After the bronchoscopy another antibiotic was added to help fight the infection and things seemed to be improving. I still had two weeks to stay in hospital now because of this new antibiotic. This would mean I would be in hospital for five weeks, longer than any of my previous admissions. I was happy though; I also knew I could not have seen it like that if I hadn't gone to Medjugorje. In 1994, two weeks in hospital was too long for me, and God and me weren't on speaking terms, well I wasn't speaking to him. Now things had changed and I thank God for that because I was now a tolerant patient.

Medjugorje had taught me so much about God's will. I just had to put my trust in God during my stay in hospital. I was meeting other people with CF, who were a great support. They had experienced similar things to me and understood how I felt. During my fourth week I was told I had MRSA. MRSA is a hospital bug that is highly infectious and resistant to most antibiotics. I was put into isolation, a room to myself to protect the other patients who were on the ward. The room had a television, VCR, refrigerator, computer and a remote control bed that moved in all kinds of positions. But after a few days the novelty of these things wore off. I missed being able to mix with the others. People with CF get to know each other and become friendly very quickly when in hospital. I think its because we're all young (thank God some are not so young now, thanks to advancement of medical treatment) and go through the same experiences.

While I was in hospital during my first week a young CF girl 'Emma' died. She was only 21 years of age. I didn't know her, but some of the other CF patients knew her well and were very upset. I've known a few CF friends who have died, but I was never in hospital when any of them died. I was experiencing something very new. I was only in hospital a few days and didn't know too many people. However this tragedy brought those of us who were inpatients closer. The hospital organised for a chaplain to come see us, to see if we were all right. Sr. Sheila met us in our CF sitting room, which is a room in the hospital just for CF patients to use. It has everything to make our stay in hospital comfortable. It has a satellite TV, VCR, books, microwave, stereo, refrigerator, a computer and three couches; it's a home away from home. Sr. Sheila lit a candle and put on some background music as she spoke about Emma, whom she knew well. There were four CF girls and myself present. We all listened and could share something if we wanted.

It was really helpful to hear how other CF patients felt. It was really a beautiful experience. I sat there with tears rolling down my cheeks listening to Sr. Sheila. I thought about my own mortality as I listened, I imagined everyone else was thinking the same. Emma was younger than me and it made me wonder about my own life's journey. I then thanked God because I have been lucky with my health over the years. Sr. Sheila comforted us with her wisdom and made us all feel very special.

She said all the people with CF she had known have a quality and ability to show love and kindness towards others, even in times when they are often very sick, sometimes sicker than the people they are trying to comfort. She told us to hold on to that quality. She said it seemed to be part of our nature. She really helped us all with our grief. I felt blessed because Sr. Sheila spoke such beautiful words of comfort. God was working through one of his angels on earth. I was glad because I did not know if the other girls were religious or not. These were words that would melt anyone's heart or even plant a seed in their heart; maybe get them thinking about God. I asked if Emma believed in God and was told "very much so". The following day we (including the chaplain) went over to the chapel for Emma's removal from the hospital to the church, for her funeral. I went to support the other girls, while inside the chapel Emma's mother called us up to her. She was standing beside the open coffin as the short service began. I had never seen someone so young dead and Emma looked like she was asleep, very peaceful. I was initially a bit shocked. (The only other person I'd seen dead was my Grandad Frank, who died suddenly in 1990, that was devastating on all the family). The priest spoke a few words about Emma and then he led a decade of the rosary. It was really hard on the other CF patients as they said goodbye to their friend. I said goodbye to Emma and asked her to pray for me now. Emma's in a better place now and that's for sure. God was teaching me more about my own life's journey.

Towards the end of my fifth week in hospital I began to feel light headed and dizzy. I thought a new drug I had started had caused it. A drug that was used to give me an appetite. They stopped that drug and the following Tuesday they said I could go home. I still felt dizzy going home but they said if it got any worse to call them. My chest infection was clear. If the dizziness got worse I would have to go back for tests. I went home on a Tuesday, however the following Sunday the dizziness was no better and I got another high temperature. So we called the hospital and they said to come back in. I spent a few days in the MRSA ward, before being transferred to St Paul's ward. They began treating me for a chest infection again. The following week my parents and brother all came down with flu. I told the doctor this, but he was convinced I had another chest infection. He started me on IV treatment again. After a week my stomach became ill, so one of my IV drugs was stopped and another added. All this was happening around March 17th, I remember this because it was St. Patrick's Day and Bryan, another CF patient in the room next to me had died. This made my mind wonder about my own mortality yet again, so much so that one night after another very high temperature. I was convinced I was going to die soon, I felt awful. I was getting three high fevers a day at least, and I couldn't take much more. I lost 14 lbs in five days. I often taught of Medjugorje and about Jesus dying on the cross during these times. I thanked God for both the joy I found in Medjugorje and for Jesus dying for my sins, His suffering out of love eased my mind. The doctors sent me for so many tests to find what was causing these high temperatures. They did a brain scan one day and thought I had Meningitis because of the results so they immediately performed a lumber-puncture. This is when they insert a needle into the base of the spine and extract fluid from the brain through the spinal cord. The results where negative, I didn't have Meningitis. Thank God, but no diagnosis was ever made. 'Suffer little children to come on to me'.

One night while I was lying awake after yet another high temperature I was listening to a cassette of the Adoration I had recorded in Medjugorje the previous June. I began to go back over the last few days to try and remember when these fevers started and to try and come up with a solution. I came up with a theory that had to be the cause of these temperatures. I was convinced they were caused by one of the IV antibiotics I was receiving three times a day. That had to be it, I thought. The next morning when the nurse came with the IV drug I told her I didn't want it until I saw a doctor. The doctor came and I told her what I thought, and she stopped the drug to see if indeed it was this drug causing the fevers. All that day my temperature stayed down until the evening when it went up to 38° C, but this was nowhere like the other fevers and was bearable. This pattern continued for days with my temperature going up maybe once or twice a day. One morning Dr. Gallagher stopped all my antibiotics to see what was causing the problem. He thought it was an infection that they could not detect yet, and without any antibiotics it would surely show up. After a week off all antibiotics no infection showed up. One afternoon I went up for another brain scan. While waiting for the scan my temperature rose again. I had no antibiotic to take down the temperature, however this high temperature passed quicker than before. I then came up with another one of my theories. I believed that my body became addicted to the antibiotic that they were giving me to take down the temperature. I felt, because I'd been getting the antibiotic so often that my body now craved them. My body temperature would rise to fulfill this craving. I told the nurses I didn't want any antibiotic when my temperature rose later that evening. I then began taking the antibiotic I would usually take if I had a temperature and within two days the high temperatures stopped. My doctor was pleased and then he talked about getting me home. However, I got another chest infection and had to start back on antibiotics for two weeks. After those two weeks my infection cleared up and I was discharged after twelve weeks and two days in hospital. This had been the longest I had ever been in hospital since I was an infant, but I got by with the help of all my family, friends, fellow patients, staff, Our Lady and Jesus. It seemed that I gave up 'home' for Lent that year, I joked.

Chapter 14

Thought I'd never get there

At the start of the year I had planned to go to Medjugorje in May. I thought it was months away, but after my stay in hospital it was only five weeks away. It's amazing what three months in hospital can do. The thoughts of going to Medjugorje had kept me going throughout my stay in hospital. I thought I'd never get there. I even found myself telling others in the hospital about Medjugorje, both patients and staff. I had a great joy in my heart as I told them how Medjugorje had changed my life. Talking about Medjugorje was keeping my spirits up, and in turn helped with my recovery. Some people listened with great interest while others 'ran a mile'. People I thought would laugh it off didn't and surprised me with their interest. They even came back and asked me more questions about Medjugorje. What was it like?, they asked. I tried to tell them, but my words were never enough. I hoped the joy, happiness I felt about Medjugorje radiated from me as I spoke. I also hoped it made them think positively about Medjugorje, maybe even plant a seed of desire in their heart to go and see for themselves.

On May 26, 1999 I left for Medjugorje with my Mam, Carla, Youlanda - a family friend we met in Medjugorje last June - and my aunt Rita, Carla's mother; it was her first Pilgrimage to Medjugorje. Rita made this trip in thanksgiving for her good health since she had cancer. Medjugorje was quiet the week we were there. The troubles in Kosovo had caused pilgrims to stay away.

Despite this the plane from Ireland was full. We stayed in a house close to the church, which was ideal for me. Our Lady was looking after me again. It also happened to be the night Manchester United the football team I support, won the Champions League Final in a dramatic finish scoring twice in the last 2 minutes of injury time. A Miracle.

I was still feeling dizzy from my time in hospital in April. The weather was very hot and caused my health to deteriorate. I was feeling a bit unwell before we left Dublin and could feel another chest infection coming on, and the heat made it very difficult for me. I found it hard walking any distance and had to rest every so often. I enjoyed the pilgrimage as best I could. I could not climb Apparition Hill or Cross Mountain. The stairs in our house was difficult enough and took so much out of me. This was my mountain. I remembered something Philip our guide said on a previous trip. He said every pilgrimage is different for every individual, some can climb the mountains and others cannot. God and Our Lady know our limits, our desires and they help us on our spiritual journey while on pilgrimage. So, we should not feel that we have to climb mountains in order to get most of our pilgrimage. Leave it in God's hands and enjoy the pilgrimage whatever happens. So, that's what I decided to do, well I tried.

The week passed by and was wonderful for all of us. My aunt Rita's faith in God was strengthened, she fell in love with Medjugorje, Our Lady and got over her fear of thunder and lighting. She received so much like so many others who've visited this wonderfully blessed village. God gifted her with many graces to go with her already very loving heart. We laughed a great deal during the week and prayed in between our giggles. God's gift of humour was a true blessing on this trip. Youlanda had us laughing at every spare moment we had.

However, I was happy to get home to the Irish weather that eased my breathing. I had a hospital appointment scheduled for the week after I returned. By this appointment, my breathing was slightly better. But my doctor was not happy with my breathing test and decided to admit me when a bed became available.

The 18th anniversary of the Medjugorje apparitions was approaching so I attended a novena leading up to that day with Mam. It was on in a university church in the centre of Dublin. Fr. Aidan Carroll was the priest giving the novena. I had noticed that there were a number of young people attending this novena. They all seemed to know each other. They must be part of a prayer group I thought to myself. However before the final day of the novena I got a phone call from the hospital to say that they had a bed for me. Unfortunately, I had to miss the final day of the novena. The novena had been lovely and I enjoyed it as much as my last trip to Medjugorje, mainly because I could breath easier.

I started my treatment immediately on a Friday just in time for the weekend. Hospitals are deserted at weekends and to make it worse it was my birthday on the 27th, so I was not too happy. However, God provided me with a magical birthday present from a total stranger. The nurses decided to celebrate my birthday by hanging up a homemade birthday banner around the curtain rail of my bed, as I slept. I woke up with these strange faces staring at me. No not the nurses! They had decorated my drip stand with inflated hospital gloves with smiley faces drawn on them. So I decided to keep them on my drip stand all day. I got some funny looks from people all day as I walked around hospital.

Later, after a good day in which I was allowed home for a few hours and after receiving loads of birthday presents, I was about to get my best present yet. After my visitors had gone home I was sitting alone in the visitors area of the hospital's main hall watching the world go by, as I do a lot to pass time during the day. It breaks up the day and gets me away from the ward for a while. Soon it was after visiting hours and the hall was empty, when along came a mother with her two children. The little girl was about six-years-old and her brother was in his buggy. They sat facing me across the hall. The little boy was not happy in his buggy, so his mother took him out. He wanted to get on the floor and explore. He could only crawl, but was an expert and travelled at great speed. He had spotted my strange looking drip stand and me. So in lightening speed he was across the hallway to me. Some visitors had to dodge him as they left the hospital. His sister was quickly over to retrieve her brother. She was helping her mother by looking after her baby brother. But before you could say, "you're not to go over and annoy that man", he was back to investigate. I love kids and kids seem to love me. (Throughout my life kids have been drawn to me no matter where I go). I was kept amused by his speed and ability to crawl. After his sister retrieved him several more times, she got curious about my drip stand too. She questioned why I was in hospital and more importantly why did the gloves have smiley faces on them. I told her I had a chest infection and she told me her grandad was in hospital. She delighted in telling me "he was coming home tomorrow". I told her that was great news, she agreed with a smile. She then touched the gloves and investigated them. I then told her it was my birthday and the nurses had put them on my drip stand to cheer me up. I wasn't crazy, and she looked relieved that I wasn't. She then ran back to her mother satisfied and told her about my birthday. The little girls' grandmother emerged from the lift down the corridor and little girl ran into her arms, inquiring about her grandad I guessed. Her brother was not far behind on all fours. They made their way towards the hospital's exit. Minutes later the little girl ran back to me and wished me a happy birthday and opened her little hand to reveal two hard-boiled sweets. I thanked her for this wonderful gift. It touched my heart so much. I waved goodbye and thanked God for the best birthday present ever. The following day I saw the little girl leaving the hospital linking her grandad's arm. She had a big smile on her face because she was taking her beloved grandad home.

I showed the night nurses the present I got from the little girl at the party they had organised for me on the ward. There were about fourteen other CF inpatients and we had a laugh. My birthday cake was distributed among all the patients on the ward. It topped of a wonderful birthday.

I was in hospital a total of five and a half weeks, as my infection took longer to clear than predicted. God's work is evident in hospital and I learned more about life and death during this stay. The following account taught me so much about my own mortality; about God's will and it strengthened my love for God - it thought me that God is with us and oversees every moment of our life, as He promised.

I was in hospital a few days when I experienced yet another CF patient's death. A young 15-year-old boy, Damien. He came into hospital and was opposite me in a six-bedded room. He was very sick on admission and the doctors worked extremely hard to make him comfortable. It was also the first week of the doctor's six-month rotation. So, the doctors who were treating Damien were very new to treating CF patients. They stabilised Damien and he had a comfortable night. Over the next few days his condition improved slightly. It was taught that he was through the worst of this chest infection. Things were looking better for Damien and he seemed to be recovering well. He even managed to get out of his bed and go for strolls in a wheelchair with his Mother and aunt.

Damien's aunt who had stayed by his mother's side since his admission decided to fly home for a few days. She'd come back at the weekend because Damien's health was improving. They lived in Kerry which is in the South West of Ireland and it was a long journey to Dublin. However, sadly and very unexpectedly the morning after Damien's aunt left for home, Damien's health took a turn for the worse. He struggled to breathe and the doctors did everything they could to ease his vary laboured breathing. The physiotherapist brought in portable ventilators to help Damien. I was looking on from my bed, as it was early morning when things changed. I took out my rosary beads and began to pray silently for Damien. While the doctors worked on Damien, Ann one of the CF specialist nurses asked me if I wanted to be moved into another room away from all the commotion. I told her I was happy to stay, I felt if Damien knew I was moving out because he was sick he would lose all hope and think the worst. The doctors worked frantically all morning with Damien and did everything possible to save him.

Sadly, Damien passed away at lunchtime. Lunch had only been served and I lost my appetite, needless to say. It still amazes me though; how some of the older patients manage to keep on eating, and look for their dessert when something so tragic is happening just feet away from them. Maybe it's just me!

I felt so sorry for Damien's mother who was all alone waiting for her family to arrive. They were contacted that morning and where traveling to Dublin. The ward sister arranged for Damien's body to be moved into a single room for privacy. The ward sister asked if I wanted to see Damien and pay my respect to his mother. I agreed and was lead into the room by a nurse. Damien's mother was sitting beside Damien's bed with one of the hospital chaplains beside her, Fr. Bryan. Damien's mother got up and embraced me and she began to cry as we hugged. I sat down beside her as she spoke lovingly about Damien. I just sat in silence, what could I say, nothing I thought. I'm not wise enough to say any comforting words. She spoke of her son and interrupted herself by saying "I can't believe he's dead". Damien looked ever so peaceful. I sat with her for about 40 minutes. I wanted to wait as long as I could. I did not want her waiting on her own too long before her husband and their other children arrived. When I left the room I telephoned my Mam and told her about Damien. Mam was shocked and came into the hospital at once. We both went into see Damien's mother. Damien's family had still not arrived, so we stayed with her. After a few minutes we heard a loud scream outside on the corridor. Damien's mother jumped up and said that it was her sister. She ran out of the room, we followed her to see if she was all right, Damien's aunt was in shock and had fallen to the floor. She was devastated; the two sisters hugged, cried and consoled each other. It was something I well never forget, it was so sad. The way the day's events transpired, made me think about my own mortality again, and how God only knows what's around the next corner in life. We know nether the hour or the day when we will meet our maker.

Chapter 15

St. Paul's Ward

I feel at this point of the book I should talk about St. Paul's ward in more detail. Since January 1999 I've gotten to know St. Paul's ward really well, so much so that I began to call it home. It's a special place. Physically, St. Paul's ward has five main rooms A, B, C, D and E all on the left hand side of the ward, with two cubicles on the right for very ill or patients who need isolation. These two rooms are both situated near the nurses station, which is situated between room C and D. The television room is beside room E and is for everyone on the ward. The CF sitting room I spoke of earlier is just around the corner from the Physiotherapy room, which is located near St Paul's ward. Many CF patients try and avoid the Physiotherapy room at every opportunity, well I did anyway. There is a kitchen situated near rooms D and E. It was always well supplied with supplement drinks for the CF patients on the ward. As a dedicated Adult CF unit it is not ideal, ideally every person with CF should have his or her own room with on suite facilities. This would help in the treatment and fighting of the many chest infections people with CF get. But Since I've been attending St Paul's this specialised unit has been promised by many governments.

I will try and describe what makes St Paul's ward such a special place as best I can. I imagine St. Paul's ward is like any other adult CF ward worldwide. Except for one major fact and that is that on St. Paul's ward there are non-CF patients too. At times this can be good and other times can be annoying. CF patients in St. Vincent's range in age from 17, 18 up to 20's, 30's and occasionally into their 40's and 50's. CF patients usually come in for two weeks of IV treatment. A pattern becomes evident of a CF patient's stay in hospital very quickly. When they come onto the ward they are usually gasping for air, or in severe pain from their lungs, stomach or other complications. They look in a real bad way, close to death one would think at times. After a few days "on the right treatment" they start to feel better and don't want to stay in bed. As a result they are up and about, making friends with other CF patients or catching up with old friends that they have known from the children's hospital. Some of the non-CF patients find this hard to understand, and it makes life difficult for all concerned at times. This is understandable as they are usually older patients who are confined to bed. They can't understand why we are up and about, if we are supposedly sick. We probably annoy them just as much by staying up late joking with the doctors and nurses, then sleeping during the day.

At times there can be any amount of CF patients in at one time. (As I write this I am only out of hospital five days, when there were twenty CF inpatients, which was an unusually high number). It can be very hectic with all those drip stands, and traffic lights are almost needed at times on the corridors. However, I have found that God works miracles through these CF patients without them realising it. Non-CF patients see all the suffering that some people with CF go through and learn more about themselves. At times they realise what they are going through is not that series in comparison. A lot of people with CF have the most amazing since of humour and that helps many of us to feel better about our own illness or situations.

There are also many sounds that make St. Paul's unique to other wards; apart from the usual hospital machine noises, bleeps, buzzes and hums. The sound of coughing can be heard twenty-four hours a day. One can even identify a CF patient by their cough alone after a while. Each cough is totally unique, as God intended. The other noticeable sound is laughter; at times painfully sore on the lungs and stomach. Laughter can be heard on St. Paul's at all times day or night, at both happy and sad times. They say laughter is the best medicine, I've found this to be true, and on St. Paul's it's compulsory as part of the treatment. Who needs a physiotherapist at these times? The laugher usually starts off a coughing frenzy, once one starts a fine chorus follows which, in turn causes more laughter.

However St. Paul's ward has another side, a side that no one likes but unfortunately is a sad reality on the ward, and that is death. Mostly when a patient dies in hospital they are at the end of a long life's journey. Life expectancy has risen in Europe and other First World Countries thanks to the wonderful advancement in science, medicine and technology. On St. Paul's however, death has a habit of coming and is quite happy to take younger lives. When a CF patient dies on the ward one can sense it instantly. No one has to say anything. Eventually, after all the CF patients who are well enough to be told about the death, the ward tends to be a lot quieter. It's a highly emotional atmosphere for a few hours. Everyone is thinking about the person who has died, their family, friends and, inevitably, their own mortality. No one really knows what to say at these times, the nurses usually leave us be, until we're ready to talk. The CF patients tend to stick together and support each other; sometimes without realising we are doing so. I often think of the staff on the ward and how hard it is for them. In most cases they have become close to the patient who has just died and they have to carry on with their work. That must be very difficult. That's why the nurses that God has sent to St. Paul's ward are a true blessing. They are very dedicated to their job; many have been on the ward for a number of years. They know us CF patients very well. Many a late night of laugher has been shared between us in the nurse's station. I'd like to take the time to thank them all now personally for their wonderful care and love for me and others.

Many CF patients are remembered on the ward with various gift donations from their families, mainly in thanksgiving for all the love and care shown to their loved ones while they were a part of St. Paul's ward. There are also many photographs on the walls of staff and patients in happier times. St Paul's ward is a home away from home, a home full of love and care by all the staff connected to it. I thank God for all the wonderful people who have cared for me, they continue to take care for others on St. Paul's ward, and are a true blessing.

St Paul's is located on the ground floor of the hospital and is the closest ward to the hospital oratory. I have found the small oratory to be an 'oasis of peace' many times. I feel very close to God when I spend time alone in there, it is so quiet, and you would never think you were in a hospital. It is a really calming space. Above the door outside it is written "Be Still and Know that I am God". The hospital also has a chapel also located on the first floor, but it's a good walk away from St. Paul's ward. When my breathing is not up to walking there, going to the oratory is easier.

Our Lady has helped me whenever I am in hospital simply by introducing me to great people. I've observed other people with CF and learned so much from them. I've made and known some wonderful friends who understand everything I go through and have gone through. We are a great support and help to one another because of this. Empathy becomes second nature to us and we really relate to one another.

As I have only recently come to know God in a deeper way. I look in awe and wonder at other people with CF who don't believe in God, and cope so well. They are so much stronger than I am; many of them have spent most of their lives in and out of hospital. I pray that they come to know God as I have, because I know their journey would be much easier with God. I've learned so much on every hospital admission; life is all about learning to love as God loves and accepting His plan for your life. God has tried to use me during all of my admissions. I say, tried, because at times I would get lazy and would not cooperate with Him. However, God has His ways of getting me to help Him. My suntan, yes my suntan was Gods' favourite way of getting me to talk about Medjugorje in hospital. I've been to Medjugorje five times as I write this, most of those times have been during the summer months. While in hospital I usually wear T-shirts and tracksuit bottoms and people see my tanned skinny arms. Also, being Irish and having a tan all year round is a miracle in itself. God does provide, Alleluia!!

Many conversations with patients and staff in hospital usually began with, "Where you away on holidays?" Most times I would say, not recently, but I was in Medjugorje a few months ago. They would say, "where?" just like I did, when I heard of Medjugorje. I would say, "it's in Bosnia Herzegovina." The usual "is that where the war is?" follows, I'd say, "it was, but its peaceful now and SAFE". "Why would you go there?" I'd explain about Our Lady and the apparitions, some would listen and question with enthusiasm, while others would say that's nice, smile with pity and 'run a mile'. At times I'd get lazy and say I was on holiday in Croatia, only because I was tired and not much company, forgive me Lord! Most times I will try and tell people about Medjugorje and when I do, I love telling them about it. The seeds are always sown when I talk to someone about Medjugorje.

Chapter 16

A New Hope

In August 1999 I was in hospital with yet another chest infection. During this admission, Dr. Gallagher, spoke to me about double lung transplantation as the next possible step in treating my illness. The reality of my illness and its progression made me think. The news that I hoped I would not hear for another few years was finally here. I always knew that one day my health would deteriorate and I would have to think about transplantation.

For years I said I would never have a heart and lung transplant. I didn't like the idea of having someone else's heart and that was my only reasoning. I can't explain it; it's the way I felt at that time. But now I was being offered a double lung transplant. I could keep my own heart if the tests proved that my heart was strong enough for the operation. Medjugorje has given me a great love of life and now I don't worry about having anyone's organs anymore, not even if tests showed I needed both a heart and lung transplant. I want to live, I really want to live. With the suggestion of lung transplantation I began to think about dying again.

I have never had a fear of dying, even as a child, I was always aware that I had to die. I understood some died younger than others, especially people with CF. I believe that this understanding and calmness about death to be one of the many graces I have received throughout my life. I thank God for this grace. For someone my age I've witnessed death in hospital on many occasions, too many at times and with people of all ages. One week four old men died in my room, I was really sick at the time and felt that I could I be next? Death seemed to be passing from one bed to the next. I began to notice the effects death had on the family and friends of the deceased.

The hardest part about dying I believe, and have learnt concerns not the person who is actually dying. But the family and friends who are affected by that death. I began to think about my family and friends. At times I would imagine those moments surrounding my own death. I felt how sad it would be for me not to see and interact with them. If I died, I wondered how would they cope, how I would cope! After living with these people for 26 years. I tend to miss them when I go on holiday, never mind on the other side. I don't know what the afterlife is like, so it might not be too long before I see my loved ones again. Who knows? I do hope and pray that I get the chance to say goodbye to my family and friends properly, if it is God's will to take me home. I'll think more about that when that time comes. For now I had to think about this new path my life was taking and deal with it 'one day at a time', as the song goes.

The influential and major factors of my new outlook on transplantation were the other CF patients that I had met on the transplant waiting list since January. They were all very positive about having a transplant, and clung to life with great hope. God placed these wonderful people in my path and they were a great inspiration to me, they made me rethink my previous thoughts on transplantation. Previously I had never met anyone on a transplant waiting list so they taught me so much. One of the Girls I got to know on the waiting list got her transplant in July 1999 and is doing great after her operation. This added to my outlook and I agreed I would go for transplant assessment. Before this I had to have several tests done. To help with my next step, I was shown a video about transplantation along with my family members in the CF councillor's office.

The only downside to the lung transplantation program in Ireland at that time was that they didn't perform the operation in Ireland. Patients had to travel to Newcastle in the North East of England. This adds to stress of the situation for both the patient and family. (Ireland's Heart/Lung Transplant unit was opened in 2003). Mam was praying that I would have my transplant in Ireland. It is all in Gods hands and so far I've accepted everything that has, and is happening to me with tremendous peace in my heart. This peace is perhaps the second best thing that God has given me in life next to my family; God has given me so much. I can't thank God enough for all He has done for me. I am a sinner, whom God loves and died for, even though at times I feel He can't possibly love me, especially when I fail to love Him. Thank God for His Divine Mercy.

Chapter 17

Deep Peace

In October 1999, while I was waiting for a date for my lung transplant assessment in Newcastle I went to Medjugorje for a week with Mam. I was out of hospital about two weeks and because I felt good I wanted to go to Medjugorje. We telephoned Marian Pilgrimages and booked the pilgrimage at the last minute. It was a great week and I was able get around more easily, without the breathlessness I had in May earlier in the year. The week was a true blessing and remains fresh in my mind to this day. On this pilgrimage, God was about to give me a precious gift that would stay with me for the rest of my life.

As I mentioned already, I love to read books and listen to audiocassettes and CD's about Medjugorje. I'm in awe at how God has touched the lives of so many others who have been or only heard about Medjugorje. One such thing I've read and heard about numerous times, and I find both beautiful and amazing, is how God works miracles through complete strangers. I believe they are angels sent by God to strengthen our belief. These are Angels who have a special message only for you, a message that no one else could possibly know.

I had only read about these encounters until this trip. God decided in all his wisdom to send me one of these angels. The following is the description of my strange but beautiful moment from God. It has reassured my faith and left me with a tremendous Peace to this day on my journey. It is one of the most real moments of God in my life. I hope by reading this you can understand why God amazes me and leaves me wondering at times, Gods ways are definitely not our ways. Thank God for that! My wondering however cannot come up with answers, so here are the facts of what happened that evening.

We arrived in Medjugorje on Wednesday night. On the Thursday evening I went down to the Croatian mass on my own after a wonderful day. Mam was already inside the church as she had left the house minutes earlier. When I got to the church it was crowded, the only space available was inside the church's doors, in the porch. I could see what was going on through the glass doors, so I stayed there. Holy Mass began and the singing was magnificent. After a few minutes I noticed a man in front of me, a middle-aged man. He seemed to be answering all the prayers in a foreign language. It wasn't Croatian, I recognise the sound of Croatian due to my previous visits. This man sung along with all the hymns, I noticed he had a lovely singing voice. As the mass went on I forgot about him until the part of Holy Mass when the priest offers us the sign of peace.

This is when God decided to give me a little sign, just to let me know that He is near me always, no matter what. When the priest said, "let us offer each other the sign of peace" in Croatian, this man I had noticed turned to me. I reached out to shake his hand; he put his right hand in mine and then placed his left hand on top of both our hands and spoke. I was so shocked with what he said that I couldn't even return the little blessing "peace be with you". When I did say something he was gone, he had turned to shake someone else's hand. I don't think he was even aware at what he'd said. The words he spoke echoed in my head and heart as I stood in disbelief. I watched him shake other people's hands. I will never forget those words he spoke to me so casually. He said, "THE PEACE OF CHRIST BE WITH YOU, KEN". I was amazed because he even paused before he said my name.

I was shocked and doubted what I'd just heard. Then I thought, I know how he knew my name. I looked down to see if I had my Pilgrim name badge on. No, I didn't have it. I couldn't understand how he knew my name. I then checked my bag on the floor to see if my name was written on it, but it wasn't. There was no-one around who knew me, whom he might have heard saying my name. I firmly believe it was the work of one of God's many angels. Afterwards I had the most amazing feeling of peace and I knew that God was close to me. I knew I would be all right - no matter what was around life's corner.

After the evening's services I met Mam in Colombo Restaurant. She was with fellow Pilgrims who were staying in our house. I told them about what had happened during mass. They all listened and agreed it was very strange. I am the first to admit it was strange at first, but it was a beautiful experience. A little moment with God that meant so much to me on my journey.

The following day I managed to climb Apparition Hill, having not been able to do so on my previous trip in May. I told God I would offer the climb up for Declan (one of my CF friends who has inspired me. He was very sick in hospital and waiting for a double lung transplant too) and for his girlfriend, who had recently lost a sister tragically. I always find that it is easier praying and doing for others. So when I made it up to the apparition site I prayed for them. I also prayed for my family and all my friends and I thanked God for the new Peace I had since my encounter at mass the night before.

Towards the end of the week my breathing began to get worse and I could not do as much as I had been doing. Mam was a bit worried, but a friend (through Medjugorje) Patricia, who is a registered nurse, was with us and looked after me. She relieved some of Mam's worries. I kept assuring Mam that I was much worse back in May.

The week passed very quickly and was filled with many memories and blessings; I even spoke to a group of young people about what Medjugorje has done for and means to me. I also found out the date for my transplant assessment when we telephoned home one day. I now had the date for the next step of my journey.

I felt that God was closer to me and believed he would be with me every step. The reality is that God is always close; it was me that was far away from him for years. I now felt ready for my assessment and its outcome. The day after we arrived home from Medjugorje I went back into hospital with another chest infection.

Chapter 18

Transplant Assessment

My appointment in Newcastle was arranged for Monday 18th of November, 1999. I travelled over by plane with my parents early that morning. We then got a taxi from Newcastle airport to the Freeman Hospital. The journey lasted about 25 minutes. After I checked into the hospital I was brought up to ward 29. I was shown my room for the next four days.

The tests began immediately with the doctor taking many blood samples. They wasted no time with the tests. The next person I met was Neil, one of the transplant coordinators. He was extremely friendly and made us feel at ease. After a few minutes talking, he asked if he could take an polaroid picture of me. It was to put in my file. They do this so they remember who's who, a face to the name. Neil then got straight down to business and began to tell us about transplantation. He did not hold back with regards to what could go wrong. He also went through the success rate and the difference transplantation would make to my life. At the end of the first day, the enormity of what was happening to me hit home. When lung transplantation was first mentioned to me it was only talk, now I was in a hospital in another country and things became very real. That first night I was thinking that transplantation was not for me. I told my parents that I'd had a good life, and that I had done many things others weren't lucky enough to have done. I strongly felt that I would not opt for a double lung transplant. However, I had three more days to go, so I decided to pray and sleep on it before I made any decision.

The next three days where filled with breathing tests, walking tests, x-rays and heart and liver echo's, as well as meeting everyone who'd be caring for me when I had my transplant. They always spoke very positively, using "when" as they spoke about the possibility of me having a transplant. Heading towards the final day I was now favouring transplantation. But, I needed some more time to think about it when I got home to Dublin. The final morning we had a meeting with the doctors, surgeon and the rest of the transplant team. They told me that I was suitable candidate for transplantation. The consultant said, however at the moment, I was not sick enough medically to go on the active waiting list at that time. But that time was coming soon. He advised me to go home and think about it. The team said they would review my situation in February in Dublin. Every few months they hold a clinic in the Mater Hospital for their Irish patients.

When I got home I had more time to reassess my thinking on transplantation, and the bottom line was if I didn't go on the list, I would die. At least on the list I would have some hope, a chance of prolonging my life. So, with the great support of my family and friends, going on the active transplant list seemed like the only step to take. Then in January, my friend Declan received his double lung transplant; this gave me great hope and belief, thank God. Others are not so lucky. I have known a friend who chose the other option because of the lack of family support they had. I found this the most heart breaking conversation I have ever had, this friend was being realistic about their situation and accepted it with courage. God called this friend home shortly after we had our conversation. This death saddened me dearly and made me count my many blessings, and I thanked God for them all. I also felt that this friend would now know and experience true unconditional love from God.

Chapter 19

The Wait Begins

At the beginning of December 1999, I was in hospital with another chest infection. At this stage I'd spent more time in the hospital than I had at home throughout the year. I got to know all the chaplains, cleaners, doctors, nurses, physiotherapists, orderlies and kitchen staff on St. Paul's ward very well. I even knew the hospital security and some of the hospital management. I found God and Our Lady were using me to either pray for, or tell people about Medjugorje. With Christmas day fast approaching I hoped to get home because every year we go down to my aunt and uncle, Patricia and Michaels house for Christmas dinner. We have done this every year since my Grandad died in 1990. It's a tradition now and Christmas just wouldn't be the same without it. So the week before Christmas my infection cleared and I was allowed home. Thanks be to God. We had a wonderful Christmas day.

As soon as Christmas day was over the big count down for the Jubilee year celebrations began, the year 2000 would be upon us. The media made a big deal of this, not because of Jesus. They had half the world scared, as they feared computers would not be able to cope with the change of date. Everywhere was on high alert.

Aaron and Paula from the prayer group; invited me over to their house on New Year's Eve for dinner. Aaron's brother Mark collected me and we made our way over. We all went to Holy Mass before we had dinner. Baby

Naomi, was now 11 months old and in very good form. She sang along with the choir as best she could. Following dinner Mark left to attend a family party to celebrate the New Year. I stayed and we said the rosary in celebration of Jesus' Birthday. We were praying as the count down to the New Year began. We finished one year and began the next in a most beautiful prayerful atmosphere. When we finished praying we hugged and wished each other a happy and blessed New Year. We then opened a bottle of champagne and toasted the year 2000. We had a wonderful night, praying and laughing together.

On January 2nd, I went back into hospital with another infection. This infection came on me very suddenly. I stayed in hospital for a week and finished the course of IV's at home. However, about two and half weeks after I finished this treatment I got another infection. When I went back into hospital my doctor did some tests and discovered that my Portacath (often referred to as a 'Port') was infected and this had caused a blood infection. A port is a small device that is implanted into chest, just under the skin. Inserting the port is a surgical procedure. I had mine inserted under a general anesthetic. Once inserted the doctors can access the main artery for IV antibiotics. The port is usually implanted as a last resort when the doctors find it hard to access veins. The veins in my arms became harder and harder to access because of all the canula's I'd had in the last year. Having discovered my port as the source of my last few infections it now meant I had to have my 'port' removed. I was a bit disappointed with this news, as I only had it inserted in September, three months ago. Maura, a nurse that I got on very well with had recommended I get one. She had told me they last for years. Losing my port meant going back to canula's in my arms for another while. If they could find any veins..!!!

When the port was removed I was put on a very strong antibiotic to kill the blood infection. I was on this for two weeks and had trouble most days as my veins broke down. This antibiotic was very strong it stung my veins with every drop. During this admission the day came for my appointment with Dr. Corris from Newcastle in the Mater Hospital.

I went over to the Mater Hospital with my Mam and my cousin Carla. They collected me from St. Vincent's hospital and we drove through the city for my appointment. In the waiting room I met Melissa and her boyfriend Harry. Melissa is a CF patient I'd gotten to know over the previous year. We've talked many times about Medjugorje and God. On one occasion I gave Melissa a small statue of 'Our Lady of Medjugorje' for her house. Melissa has a lovely lively spirit, a wonderful zest for life and has cheered others and myself up on numerous occasions in hospital. Cystic Fibrosis may attack our bodies but it rarely affects our spirit. I've met the most amazing people who've inspired and helped me to cope with my own situation and I thank God for bringing them in my life. I am very blessed.

Now sitting in the waiting room, my life had come to a new crossroad. My name was called and I was led into the room to the transplant team. Dr. Corris greeted me warmly and noted that my breathing was more laboured than the last time we met. He said the bounce had gone from my walk. He looked at my hospital chart and felt now was the right time for me to go on the active waiting list for transplantation. I was a bit shocked at first, because I remembered something the he had said in Newcastle. He said, when someone with CF is put on the list it usually means that they have 2 to 2½ years left before they die. This echoed in my head on hearing this news.

Beforehand I was hoping that he wouldn't recommend this, but I had to be realistic and accept what was happening. Afterwards, we made our way back to St. Vincent's Hospital. Inside the main door I met Nancy, another of the CF nurses. I told her that I'd be going on the active list as soon as possible. She suggested that we all go down to the canteen for tea or coffee. We went down and chatted before I went back to the ward. Back on the ward I told everyone how I got on, everyone was great. How do you feel about that was the most common question I was asked by people. The answer I gave was one I had thought about since Newcastle.

I told them, "I felt fine about going on the list." I explained that my life was no fun at the moment going in and out hospital all the time. My quality of life was not very good. Even though everyone in hospital is kind and caring, its tough going at times. By going on the list, I'd now have a chance of living longer, if I got a transplant. I also knew I may not get a transplant and I might die, but at least this way I had a chance at life.

Since Our Lady touched my heart in Medjugorje and brought me back to her Son Jesus, I feel I can cope with anything because Jesus is with me. As He promised is scripture. I thank God for this grace. Whenever I am feeling a bit low, I think about and reflect on the hymn "Be not afraid, I go before you" and it relieves my fears.

That night in hospital Therese, one of the night nurses and I chatted. Therese has worked on St. Paul's ward for many years. What she said that night encouraged me greatly and I thanked God for her words. We were chatting in the nurse's station. She was preparing the IV's for the patients on the ward who needed them. There were other CF patients and nurses present too. We were having our usual banter and laugh. When things quietened down, Therese turned to me and said, "I can't believe you". "Why? What have I done, now?" I replied. She said, "Today, you've heard life changing news and you're here laughing and joking, I've seen patients who'd be crying themselves to sleep now or looking for a counsellor." "What can I do about it, I can't change it. I'll just have to get on with it and hope and pray to God that I won't be waiting to long". I replied. God has put these special people in my life to help me on my journey; I hope I can help them in their journey. I thank God for Therese, she said what she really felt in her heart with great love because she really wanted to know if I was all right. I love Therese for her sense of fun and her wonderful spirit. She cares so much. God continues to look after me and gives me the many graces and blessings I need to cope with my journey.

Before I officially went on the active transplant waiting list, a few more tests and vaccinations had to be carried out. I also had to get my teeth checked out before transplantation. Any problems had to be sorted out before I went on the list to avoid complications after my transplant.

After transplantation I would be on immune-suppressant medication, which would mean I would have a very low immune system and could pick up infections easily. So to avoid any possible complications I had to be checked out. I went to the dental hospital and had x-rays of my teeth. The dentist who was looking after me told me, she'd never seen anything like my teeth's roots in her life. All my teeth had long roots; she showed me what normal roots should look like on another x-ray and compared it to mine. She told she was going to copy my x-rays and use it at lectures that she gave. She couldn't believe what she was seeing. I thought to myself that God surely made me the way he wanted. My dentist then checked the inside of my mouth and told me I would have to get two wisdom teeth taken out. They had not fully come up and would have to come out to avoid any complication further on. She said she would arrange with Dr. Gallagher to get me into St. Vincent's and have my them extracted under a general anesthetic. This would mean I would have to have IV's at the same time because the anesthetic would affect my chest. The next step of my journey was to wait for my dental surgery.

A few weeks later I went into hospital on a Monday morning for my surgery scheduled for the Wednesday. I was up on another ward, not my usual ward St. Pauls. I started IV's instantly, and without my port I realised how much I missed it very quickly, as the IV canuala's I was getting where not lasting long. I seemed to have them replaced everyday. I had my surgery on Wednesday morning and I well never forget the pain I felt afterwards. When Mam and Dad came into see me, they said I looked all right. Although my face was swollen and soar, Dad said he was expecting me to look worse. I think he was just being kind. I was given painkillers to ease the pain and after a few days the pain went away. The dentist came into see me a few times to check how I was healing. She told me she had a terrible time trying to extract my teeth because of my deep roots. God only knows how she got them out. She said she didn't want to damage any of the nerves that ran through my mouth. Before surgery she told me that she couldn't guarantee not damaging any of the nerves. She did her best to avoid any damage. When I spoke to her afterwards she said I might feel some numbness on the left side of my chin, as my nerve may be bruised. I told her I did feel some numbness. She said it may go away or it may not. After a few weeks it did go away, thank God.

On the Friday after surgery I was moved from the five-day ward to another ward in the hospital. There was no bed available on St. Paul's ward. However early the following week I was moved down to St. Paul's ward and into a cubicle on my own. My face was not as swollen as before, but I was still having problems with IV canuala's not lasting. So I enquired about having a new port inserted, I was having so many problems with canula's, it was getting frustrating. On the microbiologist advise it was decided I could have a new port. I was booked in for surgery to have it inserted during this admission. Unfortunately this would be my second anesthetic in two weeks, but I didn't worry because I missed having my port. No pain no gain. The surgery went well and more importantly I had a new port ready to use immediately. I prayed this one lasted longer than the previous one. With my wisdom teeth out, I was put on the active transplant waiting list officially and got my bleeper. I was now on call 24 hours a day and the wait began. I decided to pray for my donor, if it was to be Gods will that I should receive such a gift.

By this point it was now June and coming close to another birthday, my 25th. I was out of hospital, so I was happy. Mam and Dad decided to have a party at home for me and invited friends and family along. We had Holy Mass in our church beforehand. I was surprised with the amount of guests who came along; I was told it was only a small party. It was great to see everyone and we had a laugh, especially when the music came on and new dances seemed to be invented.

Daragh a friend who also has CF called into the party, we'd recently become good friends and I was glad he called. He had a good understanding of what I'm going through. In hospital Daragh has cheered me up with his many stories of his travels and his great sense of humour. He's a good friend to have and I thank God for his friendship. God has blessed me with many new friends from the hospital both patients and staff. That's what makes hospital such a wonderful place. One finds God's good work being carried out daily, both directly and indirectly.

Chapter 20

A Year and Waiting, ahuh huh.

In July 2000, I was back in hospital yet again with another infection. St. Paul's ward had just got a new ward sister, Una. She came to the ward with a great reputation; all the nurses seemed to like her. She had been a tutor in the school of nursing attached to the hospital. I met her and was impressed with her gentle and caring manner. She told me if I needed anything or wanted to know anything, just let her know. I said the same to her jokingly because I'd spent so much time in hospital since January 1999. She said she might take up my offer, as she was only settling into the job. I instantly liked Una and thanked God for bringing her to the ward. There had been many changes of staff on the ward in the previous months, so hopefully things would settle down now, less disruption.

I stayed in hospital for about a week and finished my course of IV's at home, one of the best benefits of having my Port again. I would strongly recommend a Port to anyone who maybe at that stage were they need one and are having doubts about getting one. I was only at home about a week when I got the sad news that Marie, a close CF friend of mine had died in hospital. Marie was a year or two younger than myself. Like many others, we had become good friends in recent months. She too was admitted to hospital during my previous admission. I couldn't believe the news when I heard it because I had seen Marie bounce back many times. On other occasions she actually seemed worse than on this admission. God called her home in His time. I learned a lot from Marie and realised how lucky I'd been to know her. I know God and Our Lady are looking after Marie in paradise.

The wait for my lung transplant continued and by now I'd been on the list a few months. I seemed to be getting one infection after another and things in the hospital weren't helping. In Ireland the health system is a major problem. It has no easy answers and the government doesn't seem to care enough about its people to ensure that the system runs properly. The dedicated CF adult unit in St. Vincent's hospital is in its planning stages for more years than I can remember. The government makes promises in Ireland everyday, but doesn't act on these promises. This unit will be a blessing if it ever comes to fruition. As I said earlier on, currently St. Paul's is respiratory ward on which the CF adult unit is based. At times this makes it difficult for CF patients to get beds. It seems to be getting harder and harder. It is another unnecessary worry, wondering if they have a bed when one telephones looking for treatment. I may be a little critical here because on one occasion I had a bad infection, that I felt could have been prevented from getting worse. God only knows the answer to that. A bad infection, is putting it mildly; I'll discuss just how bad it was further on. Only by God's grace did the situation improve.

One day, after feeling unwell for a few days I decided it was time to call the hospital and get sorted again. The CF nurse made an appointment to see me for that afternoon. When I saw the doctor, they decided to put me on home IV's to fight the infection. Unfortunately they had no bed. I was happy enough though; they organised home IV's and sent me home. I had to come back in a week and they would see if the IV's were fighting the infection. The following week when I went back and my breathing had improved. The IV's seemed to be working and I was sent home for another week with an appointment to see them when the course of IV's finished.

The following week I came back and felt worse than I had the week before. A breathing test proved this but the doctor was not that concerned. She explained the situation about the beds and said that they had no room at the moment. "No room in the Inn," I thought to myself. She then said I should go home for the weekend and come back on Monday to the outpatient's clinic.

Over the weekend I got worse and because I was annoyed at the doctor's attitude, I refused to go the accident and emergency department for another long wait. I felt she didn't really care. I know I was stupid by putting myself at a further risk. But I stayed at home until Monday and went to the outpatient clinic. I was so bad that a nurse unfamiliar to me saw me sitting on the corridor and offered if she could find a bed for me to lie down on. I declined her offer and said I was alright, even though I was breathless just sitting down.

When I was seen by the CF team they immediately rang the hospital's bed manager. They found me a bed on St. John's ward, which is just across the main hallway from

St. Paul's ward. They started me on IV's and put me on oxygen straight away. I was happy to have a bed and all seemed to be well until the following morning.

I got out of my bed and walked out to the toilet, which was less than 20 feet away from my bed. Mine was the first bed on the left hand side of a room with six beds, three on each side of the room. I walked out very slowly, trying not to exert too much energy. While in the toilet I felt very strange all of a sudden. I could feel my breathing getting more laboured, my chest was getting tight and I broke out in a cold sweat. I felt my oxygen saturation level was dropping fast. At this point my mind began to race as my heart began to beat rapidly, it was working extremely hard to keep me alive. I immediately thought of the king of rock and roll 'Elvis' and his last moments on this earth. I thought that I didn't want this to be the last place I visited on earth. I didn't want to be forever more remembered as the CF patient who died in the toilet. I decided quickly that I had to get out. But it was not that easy, I felt that I couldn't possibly move, as I felt very weak. I quickly prayed that God would give me the strength to get out and get help. My prayer was answered, I got the strength I needed and made my way out. I had to hold on to the wall. I managed to call a student nurse and let her know that I needed help and oxygen.

She ran to get oxygen while another nurse got a wheelchair. Actually, it was a commode, all pride and dignity leave you when you're in hospital. You just accept whatever is happening and try to be humble. They wheeled me back to my bed and into it. They took my blood pressure and oxygen saturation levels. My oxygen saturation level was very low, 53 per cent. I remember looking at the machine and thinking, "that's not right" as they rushed to put me on high flow oxygen. One of my doctors arrived within seconds. His arrival was like something out of a movie. Time seemed to move in slow motion. I was conscious throughout as they rallied around my bed. They treated it as a suspected blood clot because of my sudden loss of oxygen. Tara, the new CF nurse, arrived at my bedside after a few minutes. When I was stable, I asked her to telephone home and let my Mam know what was happening. She phoned home and spoke with Gary, he was at home from work sick. Mam was at Holy Mass. Gary went around to get Mam and let her know what was happening with me. Monica our great neighbour, since Mam and Dad moved to Tallaght in 1974 came to hospital with Mam. Dad at this time was in America continuing to do Gods work. Mam contacted him to update him on my condition, arrangements were made for him to fly home. Gary being sick stayed at home.

Mam and Monica arrived into me straight away. When they arrived the doctor and physiotherapist was just putting me on a BiPAP machine to help my breathing. The BiPAP machine pushes a constant pressure of air into the lungs. It keeps the airways open, allowing the lungs to rest a little. At first I found the face mask and the constant pressure of air very hard to deal with. It felt very unnatural. I tried to take off the mask. When I did, it felt like a concrete block was resting on my chest and my airways seemed to close up. So realising the difference between having the BiPAP on and off, it made wearing the face mask easier.

It was a very worrying time for all my family and friends. I remained on bed rest until further notice. Over the next week I began to feel a lot better and I remained on the BiPAP. I had a lot of visitors in those days. I began to think that maybe everyone thought I was going to die. My thoughts were confirmed when Fr. Albert, from our parish called to see me. He gave me the Sacrament of the sick with Holy Oil. I had thought I was dying too for one second, but that's when I decided it was best to get out of the toilet and not end up like 'Elvis'. After a number of days and now feeling much better, I was hoping to get a bed on St. Paul's ward. The nurses on St John's ward were all great, but I knew almost everyone on St. Paul's ward and staying there makes staying in hospital a lot easier. Some of the nurses from St Paul's came to visit me a few times while I was in St. John's. The Freeman hospital in Newcastle were updated on my condition throughout, and I was put on the priority list for transplantation. Dad was now home at this point, I was glad for Mam because I always seemed to get sick when he is away. After about ten days I was moved from St. John's to St. Paul's. I was happy to back where I knew everyone. As a bonus I was put in a cubicle to myself and could get proper rest at night. Pretty soon my chest infection improved and I was able to come off the BiPAP during the day. Mam and Dad came into me early in the day and stayed with me for hours on end. As I got better I told them not to come in so early. One day, jokingly, I told them to cancel the headstone. They knew I was getting better with this comment.

While in hospital I got lots of letters, cards and telephone calls from all over the world wishing me a speedy recovery. One of the most treasured of these was a message from Fr. Svet Medjugorje; I mentioned it in the introduction of the book. It was a lovely message with words of great wisdom, comfort and hope, not only for me but also for everyone who has heard his message. Dad recorded it so I could hear the message in hospital. Some of his beautiful words inspired me, the second I heard them I said that's the title of my book, "In the Moments of God" divine inspiration, I only wish it came an easier way.

Thankfully, I made a full recovery and was allowed home after about three weeks. I was home for about four weeks when I got another chest infection and had to go back into hospital. This infection was not as severe as my previous one. At this point I started to call the hospital 'home' as had I spent more time there than I did in Tallaght.

The weeks passed with me going in and out of hospital, it was my routine. Then on November 24, 2000 Dad got a telephone call that was a great shock to us all. It was news that Fr. Slavko in Medjugorje had died after finishing the Stations of the Cross with parishioners on Mt. Krizivac. He'd lead the prayers, reflecting on the Passion of Jesus Christ, after which he sat down and passed away. The news was hard to believe, I couldn't imagine Medjugorje without Fr. Slavko. He had been in

Medjugorje since 1982. Initially he was sent to investigate the alleged apparitions, because of his expertise. However, after a week in Medjugorje he firmly believed in the apparitions and eventually became the spiritual director to all six visionaries. He wrote many books about Our Lady of Medjugorje, and her messages. He did so much in the parish. The day after his death Our Lady gave her monthly message. This message was a great comfort for everyone that knew Fr. Slavko. A very unusual message, because Our Lady mentioned him in it.

Message of November 25, 2000
"Dear children! Today when Heaven is near to you in a special way, I call you to prayer so that through prayer you place God in the first place. Little children, today I am near you and I bless each of you with my motherly blessing so that you have the strength and love for all the people you meet in your earthly life and that you can give God's love. I rejoice with you and I desire to tell you that your brother Slavko has been born into Heaven and intercedes for you. Thank you for having responded to my call."

In early December I spent another week and a half in hospital. I decided to decorated my drip stand for the festive season with tinsel and flashing lights. It cheered up many people who probably had other things on their minds. As I said earlier, I have never been in hospital at Christmas and I hoped this tradition would continue. Thank God and I got out of hospital and finished the IV's at home. I had a good Christmas and New Year celebration with my family. I did what I could and enjoyed it very much. On January 6, 2001 feast of "the epiphany", (Little Christmas) My aunt Mary my Mam's sister, had a baby girl after a seventeen year gap between her other three grown children. Baby Christina, is a beautiful gift from God.

Update Note:
In August 2012 the new CF adult unit with individual rooms opened in St Vincent's Hospital. Thank God people with CF have the facilities they deserve.

Chapter 21

As I Walk through the Valley of Death

From December 2000 to March 2001 I had my best run out of hospital since 1999, eleven weeks in total. In those weeks I put on weight, which is very important for me in fighting infections. Unfortunately this run came to an end with another chest infection that resulted in a short stay on St. Paul's ward for one week, with me finishing the IV's at home.

During those eleven weeks, Dad was offered a new job that would see him work in Medjugorje for seven months of the year. Something he'd never dreamt of. It meant he wouldn't have to travel as much and would be closer to home if I got the call from Newcastle for my transplant. After thinking and praying about it Dad accepted the offer. There was great excitement at the prospect of Dad living and working in Medjugorje. It meant Mam could go over to Dad anytime that I was well enough. Mam always said she wouldn't go if I was unwell or in hospital.

Towards the end of March the day came for Dad to go to Medjugorje. It also happened to be a day ironically, when I ended up in hospital again with another infection. So Mam drove me to the hospital while Dad followed us in the car he was driving over mainland Europe with Jozo the guide I mentioned earlier to Medjugorje. Dad only stayed a few minutes, as he had to connect with the car ferry to Belgium.

During this admission another friend of mine in Michelle died. It was very sad for her parents, whom I'd gotten to know very well too. Either one of them were always with Michelle during her admissions, 24 hours a day, dedicated parents. Whenever a CF patient dies it really makes me think about my own life and mortality. I couldn't help but wonder if I maybe the next CF patient to die. This admission was the third Easter in a row that I had spent in hospital. I attended most of the Easter services in the hospitals chapel. After three weeks in hospital I went home again. At the end of April I ended up in hospital again. This time I had a very bad bowel blockage, which can also be another complication associated with Cystic Fibrosis. I was in hospital for 5½ weeks. This was a very tough admission because I was in a lot of pain for weeks. Eventually I began to feel better and was discharged soon afterwards. That summer was very hard as a number of other CF patients Linda, Andrew, Oliver and Helen all died. I knew them well from spending so much time in hospital. Through these months I talked with God a lot and hoped that my transplant would come soon. I thanked God for bringing me to Medjugorje because without it, I would not have found my faith. Without my faith, I don't think, No! I know I couldn't have coped. My life's journey seemed to be taking me through the 'valley of the shadow of death' at that time.

With the sad loss of my friends I took each day as it came and only dealt with whatever I was faced with on a daily bases. I tried to put my trust in God and not worry about what might be.

In August, my close cousin Olivia had a baby boy, Jack. Surprise, surprise, I was in hospital at the time and had to get out for a few hours to go and see him. Jack was unwell and was taken to Crumlin Children's Hospital, my old hospital. So I went from one hospital to another to see him. Thankfully, he only spent a short time in hospital and is doing very well today, he is now 11, as is baby Christina. As for me, I left hospital a few days later and had to bring a portable BiPAP machine home as the next stage of my treatment. This helped me get a good night sleep, even if I did look like an old World War 1 pilot each night. It ended the headaches I'd been waking with previously because of low oxygen levels.

My journey continued and then came September 2001 and an event that would change the world forever. Tuesday September 11th started like any other day for me, sleeping in till about 11.30am. After lunch Mam and I were just about to go and see my baby Christina, who was now seven months old. Just before we left we heard a newsflash on the radio saying that a plane had crashed into one of the towers at the world trade centre in New York City. We went in and turned on the television. As the events unfolded, the images of that day were hard to believe, they seemed so surreal; they were like scenes from a Hollywood movie. The more I saw the images the more I thought about the people in those buildings and how their day had started out as just any other Tuesday. In that moment their lives and the world had changed forever. It put my own situation into perspective. After these events I thanked God for everyday that I had. It showed me and others how life can change in a split second and how one cannot control or do anything about it. So it also proved to me that there is real evil in this world. I hope and pray all those innocent victims are with God. I've learned to trust in God and believe that everything happens for a reason. We are all part of Gods bigger plan, and learning to fit into that plan is the hardest thing in the world to do.

One good news story that happened in September, Rachel, a CF friend of mine received her double lung transplant. She was only three weeks on the active waiting list. I was delighted hearing this news. I had just spent a few weeks in hospital with her when she was put on the list. She was very apprehensive about going on the active waiting list and wondered how Melissa and I coped being on the list for so long. I know it was the grace of God that helped me cope. Thank God Rachel didn't have to wait too long. God is Good.

In October I went into hospital with another chest infection and stayed in hospital for five and a half weeks during which my second 'port' had to be taken out. One afternoon I was allowed home in between IV antibiotics. While at home I began to feel very cold and began shivering. I checked my temperature and discovered I was running a very high fever. I went straight back to the hospital. They took a blood test. When the results came back they discovered my 'Port' was infected. This meant I had to have it taken out, and meant another visit to the operating theatre. I had it taken out under a local anesthetic. I was then treated for the blood infection for a further two weeks with a much stronger antibiotic. This was a frustrating two weeks again as the IV canulas in my arms and hands kept breaking down because of my poor veins. I remember one Sunday having four canulas in the space of twenty minutes. My doctor, Ann Marie, had only called into the hospital on her day off for a few minutes. She was checking in on all the CF inpatients. We had a laugh, as she couldn't believe that the canula's went so quickly. She joked after putting in the fourth one, that she was going home no matter what. Someone else can put the next one in if this breaks down she told me. Thank God the fourth one lasted, only until Monday morning though. During the week I asked Dr. Gallagher about getting another port put in. He told me that the microbiologist said to wait about eight weeks before getting another one. He told me I could get it on my next admission, possibly.

Towards the end of this admission on November 4th a Holy Mass of remembrance was held in the chapel for all patients who had died throughout the year. Mam came along with me. After Mass in the canteen there were refreshments laid on for everyone. I saw Michelle's parents there, but I didn't get a chance to speak with them. I did speak with Helen and Andrew's mothers. Andrew's mother was trying to raise greater awareness and need for Organ Donors. Before Andrew died they were in several newspapers appealing and encouraging more people to carry donor cards. They hoped of finding a suitable pair of lungs for Andrew. Unfortunately a donor match was never found and Andrew died on July 6th. Andrew's mother was delighted to see me and asked me how I was doing. I told her how I was feeling and how long I'd been in hospital. She told me that she had a dream about me and Andrew the night before. She told me that she knew I'd be in hospital and that she had a feeling I would get my transplant. I hoped and prayed that she would be right.

After five and a half weeks in hospital I got home on November 6th. The following Friday Dad came home from Medjugorje. The season had finished and he would be home until Easter. Later that same day the four local girls from Medjugorje who work as guides with Dad, flew into Dublin. Danijela, Marija, Ozana and Vlatka came to Ireland for a charity concert Dad was giving. The concert was held in the big church on the Navan road, in Dublin. There was a 32-piece orchestra performing with Dad. I went along on the night and had a great time. I met a lot of people whom I'd gotten to know through Medjugorje. They all told me how well I looked. I told them I felt great, well as good as I could have with my dodgy lungs. Those words came back to haunt me less than 24 hours later.

The following morning I woke up and had terrible stomach cramps. I telephoned the hospital and they told me to come in straight away. Once again Mam drove me in, we used to joke that the car knew its own way to the hospital by now. Throughout the journey I was in constant pain. The doctor saw and diagnosed me and I was quickly admitted. It was another severe bowel blockage, which I'd figured already, as the pain is unforgettable. I opted to have a tube put down my nose into my stomach to help with the treatment. It saves having to drink litres of the solutions they use to unblock my system, as they taste very unpleasant. The nurses were surprised to see me back so soon as I had only been home about ten days. They were not as surprised as me, but God was planning something else, yet again. I got a bed in one of the six bedded rooms.

In the bed opposite me, there was a young CF boy Colm, whom I hadn't seen before. He seemed to be at the same stage of treatment as me, with a BiPAP machine and constantly on oxygen. It was his first admission to St. Vincent's, having transferred over from Crumlin hospital. He was a year on the active transplant waiting list. He had been called for a transplant in September, but it turned out to be a false alarm. I became friendly with Colm and his Mother. After a few days I began to feel well and began to enquire about going home. Thank God this bowel blockage was not as serious as my previous one. Before I was discharged I inquired about getting a new Port. Dr. Gallagher said to leave it until my next admission. As I had no chest infection and because I'd spent so much time in hospital throughout the year. "You could do with a break," he told me. He had hoped I'd get a good run out of hospital, maybe even to the New Year. When I told some of the nurses about waiting to get a new port, I joked with them saying, "I'll just have to get new lungs instead". So on the Friday after spending a week in hospital I was discharged, Dad collected me. On our way out, we met Julie the former CF Dietician. She told us her husband Greg was about to go on the active transplant waiting list for lungs. Julie and Greg met in hospital, Greg has CF too. After we finished chatting we made our way home. Later that afternoon Mam and myself drove Dad to the airport, as he was flying to America.

I found 2001 a very hard year because so many of my CF friends had died (six in all) and at times it left me wondering if I may be next. I accepted the fact that this was a strong possibility. I continued to put my trust in God and accepted His well; what will be will be'. At times this was hard to accept but I've learnt that God knows best. I kept hoping and praying I would get a call from Newcastle to say "Ken, we have lungs for you". Hope is a wonderful gift from God. We have a hope in Jesus.

Chapter 22

A New Day

Monday November 26, 2001 too started off like any other day for me, when I was not in hospital. I woke up about 11am, took off my BiPAP face mask then switched off my oxygen machine that hummed downstairs. This machine left a trail of green tubing leading up to my bedroom. I then had some breakfast and watched television. After breakfast I went up and had a shower. At times just taking a shower took a lot of energy out of me and it would leave me very breathless. On this day however, I felt good and enjoyed a long shower. In the afternoon the telephone rang. Mam answered it and called me saying it was for me. When I said hello the voice at the other end was that of Lynn, one of the transplant coordinators in Newcastle. She inquired how I was and said she was talking with my doctors in St. Vincent's. I did not even think about transplantation at all, sometimes I am so blind to what's going on. I just thought she was calling to chat and to see how I was doing. Yes, I know what your thinking. 'He's thick' and I admit it. The Reason they called was to say that they had found a possible donor. It should have been the first thing I thought about as soon as I heard Lynn's voice. Oh, how innocent I am at times. God wants us to be like children, but this was more childish. Lynn asked me to come to Newcastle that evening. Did she really have to ask? I began to grin as she told me this news, the penny finally dropped. Mam looking at me sitting on the stairs kept repeating "what is it? What is it?" Lynn then told me an ambulance would arrive for me at 3.30pm. This meant we had less than an hour to get ready. Our flight was scheduled for 4.40pm. Lynn told me to bring all my tablets and my BiPAP machine just in case the operation did not go ahead. When I put the phone down, I said to Mam, "we're going to Newcastle."

After nineteen months on the active transplant waiting list it finally arrived, the call we hoped would come. That's when Mam went a bit funny and couldn't think straight. She telephoned America, and tried to contact Dad. She had just missed him. He had checked out of his hotel. He was traveling onwards and was en route to the airport. We left a message that I was going for my transplant with Mattie in Boston. Mam then telephoned Lorna and Gary and told them I was going to Newcastle. I went up stairs and packed the few things I needed. A neighbour Nora came around and helped Mam pack. The telephone began to ring with people wishing me well. Good news travels fast. My aunts Mary and Rita arrived with my cousins Noel, baby Christina, Olivia and her baby Jack. Lorna arrived home, followed shortly by Gary. Lorna decided to come to Newcastle with us. Gary said he would stay and telephone more people and give them the news. I then got a phone call from one of our local priests Fr. Ben, he wished me well and said I would be in his and the whole parishes prayers. I don't know how he knew, but I didn't think about that until later. Fr. Ben has known me all my life and had baptised me as a baby. So it was nice to get his blessing on this next important phase of my journey.

The time was approaching 3.30pm when the ambulance arrived. One of the paramedics came to the front door of our house. He looked in and asked who the patient was, as their where so many people in the house. I identified myself to him and we were ready to go. We said goodbye to everyone. They all waved us off as we climbed into the back of the ambulance.

As the ambulance pulled away, I wondered if I'd ever see home again. On the motorway to the airport I telephoned St. Paul's ward to tell them I was on my way to Newcastle. I spoke to Tria, the newest ward sister and she was delighted for me. She asked me to get Mam or Lorna to contact the ward if the operation was going ahead, because we still didn't know at that stage if the operation would go ahead.

We arrived at Dublin airport and went straight out to meet the private plane that would take us to Newcastle. When Mam saw the plane she began to panic, because she hates flying and the plane was tiny. There was only enough room for three sitting passengers and it had a stretcher bed. The pilot looked very young, about twenty years of age, which in fact made Mam feel worse. Soon, we were airborne and on our way to Newcastle. It was a lovely calm sunny day, the blue sky stretched for miles and the flight went very smoothly. Mam sat staring at the floor and praying to herself. Lorna and myself were highly amused by her as we thought she was speaking in tongues. We could only hear her mumbling to herself. Half an hour into our journey, Mam got brave and looked up, only to see the pilot looking at a map. She immediately panicked saying 'He doesn't even know where he is going', and began to look at the floor again and pray harder! She really kept Lorna and myself entertained the whole duration of the flight.

We touched down in Newcastle at 4.50pm and were met by an ambulance. Within ten minutes we were at the Freeman Hospital. I was taken straight for a chest x-ray and then brought up to ward 29 where I had bloods and MRSA swabs taken. We then met Neil, the first transplant co-ordinator I had met two years previously, he told us that we would know if the operation proceed at around 9pm. We had a long wait. This wait was worse than the previous nineteen months, as I was so close to having the operation. If the transplant didn't go ahead I wondered, how would I feel?

At 9pm Neil came back and said we wouldn't know for another hour, the team retrieving the lungs hadn't arrived at their destination yet. At 10pm he came back and said the donor lungs looked good and the operation was going ahead. I was so pleased upon hearing this. Things then happened very quickly and I was brought straight down to the operating theatre. Mam and Lorna came into the pre operation waiting area with me. We were asked if we would like some time alone, I declined the offer and I joked with Mam and Lorna saying, "I'll see you on the other side".

We said our goodbyes, hugged and kissed. I was then lead into the pre operating room where I had a canula put in my hand, eventually, after many efforts to find a vein. Within ten minutes I was asleep. I must have been the happiest person ever wheeled into an operating theatre. I couldn't stop smiling. I repeated to myself "Jesus I trust in you", as they sent me off to sleep.

The next thing I remember was waking up in the intensive care unit with all my family standing around looking at me. Hurray! I was not dead. I thought it was Tuesday, but it was in fact Wednesday. The operation had lasted about eight hours and I had made it through the critical 24-hour period. Gary informed me that 'Robbie Fowler' (soccer player) had signed for Leeds United. I immediately began joking with my family. I was hooked up to so many different machines and had four chest drains coming out, two either side. The nurse caring for me was surprised with my sense of humour. He asked, "Is he always like this?" I was only waking and coming round when Lorna and Gary began taking photographs of me. I said, "One for the Memorial card" as I posed, to the nurse's shock.

Things moved rapidly and by that afternoon I was moved out of intensive care up to Ward 27a, the transplant ward in the Freeman hospital. I had a cubicle with an en suite toilet and shower. I was monitored all of Wednesday evening, having my blood pressure and oxygen saturation levels taken every few hours. Later that evening the doctors took me off the oxygen to see how my breathing was unaided, because my blood gas levels were good all day. After an hour, my oxygen levels were still 100 per cent on room air, so I didn't need oxygen again. In my room there was a telephone on the wall at the end of my bed. It soon began ringing. It was relatives and friends enquiring about me. They were wishing me well and a speedy recovery. Mam would answer the phone and tell them how I was doing. She would then say "hold on" and hand the phone to me, I would say "hello" and give whomever on the other end of the line a big shock. They had not expected to hear from me so soon. Lorna and Gary had flown home after a few days, they both had to go back to work. Gary took the photographs of my new scar with him; he wanted to show everyone at home how I looked after the operation. My scar is just under the breast bone from one side to the other.

Over the next few days I improved greatly and was walking around the cubicle by the weekend. I was still in a lot of pain, and I now had two chest drains left draining fluids out of my chest cavity, but my pain was well controlled with painkillers during the day. At night it was always worse. During the day I could press a button to get pain relief but because I was not pressing it enough at night I always woke in terrible pain. I could never get comfortable at night. Some nights I would have to get out of bed very early and sit in my chair just to get some pain relief. Gradually they reduced the amount of painkillers they had to give me. After a week they did a bronchoscopy to see how my new lungs were, they where looking for any sign of rejection. Thank God there was no sign of rejection. This meant I could now go to the gym and do some exercise.

They wasted no time in helping my recovery. During exercise there was no problem with my breathing, the only problems I had was with the muscles in my legs and my back. The reason for this was, that before the operation I could not do any exercise without getting breathless very quickly. Even getting dressed some mornings made me very breathless. This had left my leg muscles very weak. My back muscles began to hurt as I was now walking upright. Before the operation I was stooped over because it was more comfortable for me and helped my breathing. These pains lasted a few weeks before I got stronger.

After a week I had my first visitor from home. It was Michael a neighbour of ours who was on business in Newcastle. Michael is the group leader from my second visit to Medjugorje. It was great to see and chat with Michael. Being away form home was very hard on my parents, not having the full support of family and friends. I didn't mind that much, I was happy to have my new lungs.

I was doing really well and after ten or eleven days the surgeon came into the room and asked me when was I going home. Later that day they began discussing discharging me to the hospital apartments for the rest of my stay in Newcastle. They like to do this with patients who are from out of town so that they can monitor them before fully discharging them. They arranged for me to move over the following Monday, because I was still in a lot of pain, they decided to keep me until Monday. On Saturday morning, we (Parents and Myself) were sitting in my room looking at the television when one of the nurses stuck her head in the door and said we had some visitors from Dublin. It was my aunts, Dad's three sisters Betty, Patricia and Rita. It was such a surprise to see them and great to chat to other people. On Monday I was discharged to the apartment for the rest of my stay in England.

I stayed in the apartment for two weeks. During this time my cousins Carla and Linda flew over to see me. They stayed overnight and then flew home. It was really great to see them. The following weekend Lorna, Gary, Cyrelle (Lorna's boyfriend) and Monica (neighbour) all flew over to see me. The second hardest part about having the transplant in Newcastle was being away from all my family and friends. I'd never appreciated how lucky I was before in Dublin to have so many visitors. The hardest part was the actual operation, but you've probably gathered that already. Thankfully since my operation, Dublin has a heart and lung transplant unit. It was opened in the Mater Hospital in 2004 and it performed its first double lung transplant in January 2006. Please God many more transplants will take place in the coming years and many CF patients will get a new lease of life.

While I stayed in the hospital apartment I continued to go to the gym every morning for exercise. I also had to visit the outpatient's clinic to get use to the hospital for when I'd return as an out patient for my checkups. While at one of the clinics the senior nurse, Mary told me that because I was doing so well and because Christmas was less than a week away, I might get home for Christmas. She said she would provisionally book three airline tickets home on Christmas Eve. This was great news; usually Irish patients have to stay for a minimum six weeks. But before going home I had to have another bronchoscopy. This took place on Friday the 21st December. When the results came back I was told there was slight rejection. I then had to stay in hospital for a course of steroids over the weekend. I feared I would not get home for Christmas, after building my hopes up. However, on Saturday Dr Corris my consultant came into see me and said I would still be going home on Christmas Eve if there where no major problems. I felt much happier with this news.

That Sunday night I could not sleep at all, I felt like a child waiting for Santa to come on Christmas Eve. I was so excited at the thoughts of going home and seeing everyone, I just couldn't sleep. On Monday morning I had to go to the clinic again. All was well and I got the all clear to fly home. However, I had to return to Newcastle in two weeks time, but I didn't mind, as long as I got home. After the clinic we thanked everyone for caring for me and made our way over to the apartment to pack up everything. We ordered a taxi to take us to the airport. While waiting on the taxi I went back up to ward 27a with the key to the apartment. I said goodbye and thanked them for all they had done for me. I told them that I would see them in two weeks. I wished them all a Happy Christmas and New Year.

The flight home took about an hour and before long we had touched down in Dublin. As I looked out the window of the plane a few tears came to my eyes. I thanked God I was home and realised how blessed I had been throughout the surgery and my speedy recovery. It was not even four weeks since my operation. Lorna, Gary and Cyrelle met us in the airport. Cyrelle drove us home, as we turned the car onto the road to our house,

Lorna asked us if we noticed anything. We didn't at first, because it was dark, our neighbours had tied yellow ribbons around the trees of our estate to welcome me home. That night many neighbours and family called in to see me. At times I was running up and down the stairs, just because I could now. It was the best Christmas present I could have wished for, to be home for Christmas with all my family and friends. "For the mighty God has done great things for me…. And Holy is his Name".

On Christmas morning we got up early and exchanged gifts. At 10 O'clock all the family went to the children's Holy Mass, as we have done every year, except me. I could not attend, as I had to stay away from public places and crowds for six weeks. This was to prevent me picking up any infection,because of the high dose of anti rejection drugs I was taking.

After Mass many more relations called in to see me, it was great to see everyone. They could not believe how well I looked now and commented on how much taller I seemed to be, I'd just straightened up. In the afternoon we were going to my aunt and uncle Patricia and Michael for Christmas dinner, as usual. On the way I stopped at St. Vincent's hospital and ran into the see everyone on St Paul's ward, my home for practically the last three years. I decided to go in on my own while the others waited in the car. As I walked onto the ward all was quiet. The first nurse I saw was Aileen, she couldn't believe her eyes and got very emotional. She gave me a big hug and then she started to cry. The other two nurses I know were on their lunch break, so Aileen telephoned down and told them I was on the ward. Within minutes Orla and Sue came up and it was hugs all around. Then two of my doctors, Ann Marie and Shane, who were on call, came into the nurse's station. They couldn't believe that I looked so well and that I was home so quickly. They questioned why I was on St. Paul's. I told them that I had to come and see them because of all they'd done for me. I knew that the ward would be quiet, and that no one wants to work on Christmas Day. I hope I cheered them up because the work they do is priceless, and nothing I can say well ever convey how thankful I am to them all for their love and care.

Christmas 2001 was the best ever for all my family and me, but for the family of my donor it must have been the hardest. I thank God everyday for them and their wonderful precious gift of life.

Donor awareness is something that needs to highlighted more in Ireland and elsewhere too. I would appeal to everyone reading this book to talk about organ donation with your families and friends. If you have already decided to donate your organs or are thinking about doing so, please make sure you inform your next of kin of your wishes, because they have to give the final consent. Think about this, organs can only come from someone who is on a life support system, and whose brain stem is clinically dead. So please be aware of this fact. The recent scandal about organ retention in England had a dramatic affect on the amount of transplants being performed. I was only the second Irish cystic fibrosis patient in 2001 to have a double lung transplant and I know of at least eight people with CF who died in 2001, most of them were waiting on a transplant. So you can see the ratio was not very good only one in five got transplants. That's why I'm going to be blunt and say to you, what good are your organs to you when you die? You can help so many people, who at this moment are waiting for organs. People are dying waiting for Kidneys, Livers, Hearts and Lungs. Others are losing their eyesight waiting for new Corneas. So please think about being an organ donor now, it's a wonderful gift to give anyone, the Gift of Life.

Chapter 23

Returning to Medjugorje

In the year after my transplant I have returned to Medjugorje four times. The first trip was a real trip of thanksgiving and I found it hard to believe that I was back and thanked God for the new gift of life once again.

Just before my second trip back to Medjugorje I was in Newcastle for a check up. I enquired and found out details about my donor. I was given my donor's name and that he was a 20-year-old boy from Ireland who had died of Meningitis. So while in Medjugorje I prayed for him and his family. On my next visit to the hospital I gave them a letter I wrote in thanksgiving. The hospital passed it on to my donors' family. I have not heard back from his family. I hope they took some comfort from my words of thanksgiving and my understanding of the loss that they suffered.

During this pilgrimage I met some wonderful people. I became friendly with a girl from Dublin, Michelle, on the second last day of her trip. I still had another week before I travelled home. She was in Medjugorje for the first time with her parents, her younger sister Ciara and family friends. Pat, Michelle's Dad and his friend Niall got to stay another week and I got to know them better during their extra week. When we were all going home after our second week, I got Michelle's address so I could keep in contact with her. I told Pat that I would send him some audio recordings I had made during our time in Medjugorje. I sent them to him a few days after I got home. I put a small note in the package for Michelle. I included my phone number and address if Michelle wanted to contact me. I had remembered how isolated I had felt after my first trip to Medjugorje.

A week after this trip to Medjugorje, my Mam's Mother, 'Nana Kathleen' got very sick and was taken into hospital. Mam was still in Medjugorje and was scheduled to come home the following morning. Nana was very sick and things didn't look good. Mam flew home as planned. We never told Mam how sick Nana was until she got home; we didn't want to worry her. Especially since she was flying home on her own. Lorna collected her and they drove straight to the hospital. All Mam's brothers and sisters were there, all seven of them. They were told that Nana was dying. That afternoon I went down to the hospital. At one point Mam, myself, my aunt Rita, her daughters Olivia and Carla, were in the room with Nana. We decided to pray the rosary for her, we prayed that she would have a peaceful death. Nana was very agitated. While saying the rosary Nana became very peaceful. I knew she was nearing her last breath. We then went outside for a break and Mam telephoned Dad in Medjugorje. While she was on the phone, we got word to go back into Nana. When we arrived Nana had just passed away with most of the family around her. Later in the afternoon, I was alone in the room with Nana. I began to talk to her I asked her "now that you're with God ask him about sorting Melissa out for her transplant". Melissa had been waiting for over two years for her transplant. Nana

Kathleen was now in Heaven with my Grandad Tommy, he died a few years before I was born.

The following day I was at home and I got a message on my mobile phone. I had two missed calls, one call from an English number and mobile I didn't recognise. So I sent a text message to the mobile that I didn't recognise and got a reply from Sammie, another CF patient. She was letting me know that Melissa was undergoing her transplant at that very moment. I was delighted upon hearing this news. I remembered what I had asked my Nana Kathleen, she wasn't long in asking God about Melissa. I called Mam immediately who was down in Nana's house and told her about Melissa. She was delighted as she knows Melissa really well too.

Mam let everyone know as some of my aunts know Melissa too. It cheered up the rest of the family and they all enquired about Melissa and how she was doing over the following days. It was news that helped everyone in dealing with Nana Kathleen's death. Michelle also contacted me on the day that Nana died. She was sorry to hear my sad news and said she and her family would pray for us all. Since then Michelle has become a very good friend of mine and to my family too.

In October on my third trip post transplant to Medjugorje I achieved something I hadn't achieved since 1998. I climbed to the top of Mt, Krizivac, Cross Mountain. I had tried to climb it on my first trip after my transplant in April. I only made it to the seventh station of the Cross then. This time I thanked God when I got to the top and prayed for everyone I know. I prayed at the spot where Father Slavko died in November 2000. Looking at the stone plaque placed there with his image on it, I found it hard to believe that he was dead. I also felt blessed because I remembered the many times that he led the prayers at Adoration in Medjugorje. I also remembered the early morning on cross mountain in 1997 when Fr. Slavko passed me on the mountain on his way up. This third trip was over all too quickly. Gary and myself had to go home, Gary for work and me for a hospital appointment. I also got back for the final week of Dad's working season in October. It was a great week, one I spent with Regina from Galway and many other group leaders who where on a special pilgrimage organised by Marian Pilgrimages celebrating 10 years in business. We had such fun on this trip, we seemed to laugh all week in between all the prayers of course, needless to say.

Chapter 24

A Mothers Love

This chapter is for the person who has had the biggest impact on my life, my Mam. After my first trip to Medjugorje, and experiencing the love of Our Lady. I began to think of something that I heard someone say on that trip. They said Our Lady loves us more than our earthly Mother. I began to really think about these words in relation to my own Mother. I thought of all my Mother had coped with between me and my Dad's illness. She has such a strong faith, love and belief in God. She believed everything would work out as God intended. At times I find it hard to believe that anyone could love me more than Mam. But our Heavenly Mother Our Lady does, and that is why I thank God for blessing us with a wonderful Mother. I look forward to meeting my Heavenly Mother, as I am blessed to have such a loving Mother here on earth. I presume everyone feels the same about their own mother, and that makes Our Lady's love for us even more awesome. To think, that Our Lady loves us more than our earthly mother? It's hard to comprehend. It makes me smile when I think how much love that could possibly be. I thank God for His mother and my mothers love. I am truly blessed. I also have many other 'Mammy's' who look out for me, you know who you are..!!!

The following is a letter I wrote to my mother, Anne, when she was going to Medjugorje in June 2001. It was just five months before my transplant. I was at home at the time and doing ok, so Mam could travel to

Medjugorje. Before she left I wrote a letter, placed it in an envelope and sealed it. I put it in her suitcase without her knowing. On the outside, I wrote, "Mam, to be opened at the Blue Cross". So here is what she read when she opened the letter at the Blue Cross.

Well Mam,

You're probably wondering what I want you to read here at the Blue Cross! So here it goes.

It's nearly four years since I went to the Blue Cross and the Statue of Our Lady, wondering about life. Wondering about who I am and why I had Cystic Fibrosis. As my mother you always made me feel no different to anyone else. "The truth will set you free". But as life went on, my mind lost the love of God that you and Dad had taught us as kids. After the many twists and turns life takes, your prayer for me was about to be answered. I thought for myself and about myself and thought I was happy until I went to Medjugorje.

As I sat close to where you are now, that day in July 1997, I was listening to the birds chirping (your Medjugorje Swallows) with the morning sun bathing me. I waited for Philip and Fr. Joe to talk and give their reflections. Little did I know that Our Lady was about to introduce me to God. As they both spoke I realised God had made me the way I am and he hadn't made a mistake. He could have easily given me normal lungs, but he had a better idea. I have learnt in the past two and a half years that I am so lucky to know God's love. They say your health is your wealth but your faith is better than that. The peace I have in my heart is the best grace I received in Medjugorje. That's why I'm in no rush to go back. The many prayers and Masses offered up for me around the world play a bigger part in my peace. Many times I forget to pray or even acknowledge God and Our Lady, so these prayers help.

God and Our Lady have always looked after us where Medjugorje is concerned; with the many good friends we have met and continue to meet. So enjoy your week and pray for those who don't know God's LOVE. Enjoy the week away from St. Vincent's hospital and me. Laugh and Pray hard!

I thank God for you, Dad, Lorna and Gary everyday, and for the rest of our family. I look forward to going to Medjugorje with my new lungs, in God's time. Bye for now and see you soon.

Ken, June 2001

I felt such peace writing this letter, the words seemed to flow with ease, much like writing this book. I had complete trust that God was with me no matter what was to come, a beautiful gift. Some of the things I've written in this book have surprised me; Our Lady and God seem to be guiding every word that I write. My English teachers would be surprised to be reading a book written by me, I was never very good at English in school, and the first English Exam I passed in secondary school was my Intermediate Certificate in 1990. So God must know what he's doing, because I haven't a clue at times.

Everyday while I was in St. Vincent's hospital my Mam would come into me, most days twice. Some days we wouldn't even talk that much. Just having her there was a comfort and we didn't need to talk. A mother's love goes beyond words. Her loving presence was enough; actions speak louder than words, as the saying goes. Just as in Medjugorje, most people experience Our Lady's Motherly presence, without her actually speaking or physically appearing to them personally, they experience her love and are comforted. Sometimes in life words are not needed and just being there for others is enough. Jesus was always there for others when he walked from village to village. His life is an example to us as to how we should live. When Jesus was dying on the Cross He gave us His Mother to love and care for us all. This motherly love is a wonderful gift that is to be cherished always.

Chapter 25

Friends Forever

Before I finish this book I would like to remember my CF friends who have gone home to the Lord. Throughout the book I've mentioned some of them by name. But I only really mention them around the time of their death and don't go into great detail on the journey of our friendship. I should have, because those stories could fill books on Friendship, Love, Pain, Laughter, Tears, Sorrow, Joy, Hope, Faith, Brotherhood, Sisterhood, Angels and God's Love. If St. Paul's ward could only talk, it could tell some amazing stories that would sound like the strangest fiction and the most wonderful, amazing story of God's love. Each of the friends I've been blessed to have known, have all been placed in my path to teach and inspire me on my own journey.

Many nights we chatted in the nurse's station and at doorways of rooms. We all helped each other on our own individual journeys, most times without even realising it. We are a community that help one another. We experienced many of the same things, and could always comfort one another when things didn't go too well. Talking and comparing notes (not literally, if any doctors are reading this) always helped and relieved fears.

I can't finish this chapter without talking about all the doctors, nurses and other personnel who have passed through St. Paul's Ward. They became good friends too, people like Julie, the bubbliest dietician who lit up the ward with her infectious laughter. People who've all made life a lot easier, and they too, have to deal with losing close friends. God blesses them and will reward them for their excellent and dedicated work. I will never be able to thank them enough for all they have done for me and continue to do for others. God Bless you all, you know who you are and more importantly God knows who you are!

In August 2003, I came home from Medjugorje after eighteen days. While there I was asked to speak briefly at a youth prayer meeting. Just minutes beforehand I learnt that Nadia, another close and good friend of mine had passed away and gone home to the Lord. I was in shock as I spoke, but I felt that Nadia was looking after me, probably laughing at me! When I got home to Ireland I got news to say another friend Robbie was not doing so well. Sadly Robbie joined the Lord a few days later. too Robbie was 34 years of age and was very well known to most people with CF, as he worked for the Cystic Fibrosis association of Ireland. Robbie's death was a shock to everyone who knew him. I have many happy memories of both Nadia and Robbie that fill me with joy when I think of them.

Finally, I would like to talk about Melissa. I spoke of Melissa earlier in the book and how she had a double transplant the day after my Nana Kathleen died. Sadly, in February 2003, Melissa went home to the Lord. Unfortunately her transplant didn't turn out how we had all hoped. Melissa had no regrets about having the operation. We spoke about this the week before she died. Melissa and I became very good friends over the few years we'd known each other. We spoke many times about God and Our Lady while in hospital, mostly when Melissa couldn't sleep and wanted someone to chat and keep her company late at night. We chatted for hours about anything and everything, Melissa had a great spirit and I miss her very much. Heaven must be full of my CF friends cheering everyone up, because on earth they certainly did a lot of that. I miss them all but we'll meet again, please God!

I would like to remember some of my CF friends by name; God has placed them in my life and I've been blest to know them. Most of them I knew very well and the others, I was not so lucky enough to have known that well, because I only knew some of them a short time.

Paul, Barret, Davin, Emma, Bryan, Ciara, Damien, Marie, Linda, Michelle, Andrew, Helen, Oliver, Alex, Theresa, Georgina, Melissa, Fiona, Laura, Nadia, Robbie, Rachel, Michael, Eoin, Sharon, Sammie, Stephen, Jane, Jean. Daragh, Mikey, David and Fiona. Rest in peace.

Chapter 26

Pure In Heart

God has continued to bring me on a journey. A journey I would never have chosen for myself. God has a better plan for our lives, better than the one we have planned for ourselves. God has taken me as far as California, twice, to do his work. The first time I went, I was suppose to speak at a conference, but I wasn't ready to do so. However, the following summer during my tenth trip back to Medjugorje in August 2003, God and Our Lady helped with this. In those days they gently guided and prepared me for my second trip to California in October later in the year. In Medjugorje I spoke in front of the small group that I mentioned in a previous chapter briefly; this confirmed what I felt I was being called to do, tell people my story. After this, I learnt to trust the Holy Spirit, and He helped me to speak in front of 2500 people at the Medjugorje Peace Conference in Irvine, California. The Holy Spirit helped me through my fear. In His time God gave me the courage and understanding to do His work without any worry.

God then brought me into contact with two prayer groups in Dublin that continue to help me grow spiritually, they are Youth 2000 and Pure in Heart. Both these groups have given me the best friends anyone one could wish for. They are a true blessing and an answer to prayers. To all involved in these groups, I thank God everyday that you are all a part of my life. I pray that God continues to bless you all.

I would like to tell you more about Pure In Heart because it has become a major part of my life. While in Medjugorje in August 2003, I met three girls from the group Angela, Edel and Janet. They invited me along to the prayer meeting some Thursday evening when I got home to Dublin.

A few weeks after I got home I decided to go to Pure In Heart. When I arrived at the house in Ballsbridge, an area of Dublin, Angela and another girl called Mary warmly welcomed me. It was good to see Angela again and I instantly felt at home with the group. That night was the first night of a 'Life in the Spirit' seminar that the group were running. The seminar is based on the gifts of the Holy Spirit. The seminar was over a seven-week period. I decided I would do the seminar, so I returned to Pure In Heart each week. All these years later, I continue to attend the prayer meeting every Thursday. I know that Our Lady led me to this group to teach me how to love God and others with a pure heart. I'm still learning to do this. I have made so many great friends in the group and feel truly blessed by God. What really attracted me to the group was the prayerfulness before the Blessed Sacrament. At present we pray the Rosary, Celebrate Holy Mass with some time before the Lord in the Blessed Sacrament afterwards. We finish the prayer meeting with a teaching on the groups charism. Afterwards we have a chat over a cup of tea.

Pure In Heart originated from a Medjugorje youth prayer meeting based in University Church in Dublin that started in the late 1980's with Fr. Aidan Carroll as spiritual director. The same church I attended the Medjugorje Novena, when I saw the group of young people back in 1999. Pure In Heart is much more than a weekly prayer meeting though.

Pure In Heart is an Irish Catholic youth community dedicated to promoting the virtue of chastity. It was formed after the inspirational and challenging words of the late Pope John Paul II at World Youth Day Rome, in the year 2000. Pure In Hearts mission is to educate, inspire and empower young people to live pure and chaste lives. Pure in heart has a mission team that speak in secondary schools, at youth retreats, and in parishes throughout Ireland giving retreats, multimedia presentations and workshops.

In September 2005, I began working full-time with Pure In Heart alongside two others, Damian and Rob. The community has really grown in recent years. There are about ninety young people now who belong to the community in Ireland. On September 21, 2006 a second 'Pure In Heart' prayer meeting was set up in St. Catherine's oratory on the Maynooth college campus in County Kildare. This has been a very exciting development for all of us involved with Pure In Heart.

Pure In Heart is trying to help young people throughout the country understand the meaning of their sexuality. In today's society and media, young people are only getting one message about sex and it is not a good message. In the name of freedom and choice many young people are feeling and experiencing the complete opposite. They are worried about all kind of things like pregnancy, sexually transmitted diseases, feelings of being used... etc. The list can go on and on. The work is plenty but the labourers are few, springs to my mind when I think of the enormity of Pure In Hearts mission. But I thank God for all the young adults who are led to Pure In Heart. Many have been inspired to really get involved in the mission.

In our work we tell the young people that God did not designed Man and Woman for multiple sexual partners. Sex should be kept for marriage, it works best in the safety of marriage. Pure In Heart draws on the Catholic Churches beautiful teachings. Pope John Paul II was a great prophet and man of wisdom in this area. Early in his pontificate he gave reflections every Wednesday at his audiences in St. Peters Square on the subject. These reflections lasted a number of years and where put together in to a body of work called 'Theology of the Body'. These reflections will revolutionise the way the people relate to each other and respect the dignity of others.

Pure In Heart as a community is constantly learning about purity of body, mind and heart. We are trying to perfect our love, so that we will be with God one day. In St. Mathews gospel in the bible Jesus says, 'Blessed are the Pure In Heart they shall see God'. (Mat 5:8) This is and should be everyone's aim. The best way to ensure that we see God is to be Christ to others. Please keep Pure In Heart and its mission in your prayers. There are three young adults working with Pure In Heart currently. Pure In Heart relies on God's providence, so I ask you to support the mission with your prayers and donations.

Chapter 27

Camino de Santiago de Compostela

One sunny day in may 2007. I was walking to a shop with Rob and Elaine, near the Pure in Heart office. We were talking about our plans for the summer. Rob was telling us, he was thinking of doing the Camino de Santiago walk again. The Camino de Santiago is the pilgrimage to the Cathedral of Santiago de Compostela in Galicia in northwestern Spain, where legend has it that the remains of the apostle, Saint James the Great, are buried. Rob had walked it alone the previous year for two weeks, and wanted to experience it again. As he was talking about his plans, he spontaneously asked, if I would like to join him. At first I thought this was a crazy idea. Rob knows that I am not the most active person in the world, so I thought it was strange that he should ask me to do such a thing. However, I was curious and enquired when he was planning his trip. He said he hoped to walk for three weeks, arriving in Santiago on July 25th. When I heard this, I really began to think about going. July 25th is the feast day of Santiago (St James), and this year, it will be my tenth anniversary of the beginning of my conversion in Medjugorje in 1997. I told Rob I would pray and think about it and let him know.

Over the next few days the pilgrimage was all I could think about. I really knew in my heart that God was inviting me to go. I knew that God would take care of me if I decided to do so. I knew that I would be safe with Rob. In deciding, I had to take my first step forward in complete faith. I was ready for this new adventure and would do the pilgrimage in thanksgiving for my ten wonderful years of discovering God, His love, and the gift of my second chance at life; that He has so generously given me. When I informed Rob that I was going, he was somewhat surprised, but looked forward to our journey. My Mam thought I was crazy when I told her of our plans. When I explained to her that Rob had done the pilgrimage last year, she really thought he was crazy too. But I convinced her that we were not crazy. She was concerned for my health. I insured her that I was physically able for the journey. We had to trust that God would take care of me; He has done so much for me thus far, so what's a few hundred kilometers walk!!!

I booked my flight to Biarritz in France for July 4th. I didn't really research much about the pilgrimage. I got advice from Rob, stuff he had learnt from his experience last year. He told me to travel very light and he gave me a list of the essentials for our journey. So in the weeks leading to our departure I got what was needed. Here is a tip for those planning on walking the Camino de Santiago de Compestela. Packing should be kept to the minimum, because carrying a bag on your back kilometer after kilometer gets tougher with every step.

The weeks past quickly and by the end of June I had finished working with Pure In Heart. It was time for Damian, Rob, Elaine and myself to move on and make way for the new mission team, who had been training all month. I thank God for them. They have a great zeal for the work ahead of them.

The day before our departure, Rob and Myself met in Dublin city centre to buy a few last minute things. In town, we met with Francesca an Italian girl from Sardinia. She has been living in Dublin learning English since August '06. We got to know Francesca after she came along to a retreat that Pure In Heart and Youth 2000 had organised in April. The retreat was a celebration of the life of Pope John Paul II, the wonderful writings and teachings he has left the Church, especially his work titled 'Theology of the Body'. Francesca has been attending the Pure In Heart prayer meeting in Ballsbridge since that retreat. I didn't really know Francesca because I was attending the prayer meeting in Maynooth. We met with Francesca to get to know her a little better. She and her friend Cristina, who lives in Italy, had arranged to go on the pilgrimage to Santiago too. By coincidence they had organised for the exact same dates and were starting from the same town in France. Looking at it now, it is clear that it was no coincidence, but a God-incidence that we should all journey toward Santiago de Compostela together.

Our departure day came and I met Rob early in the airport. This would be the first portion of a busy summer of pilgrimages. After our three weeks in Spain, Rob and myself would be home in Ireland for three days and travel down to Knock Shrine, County Mayo. We'd attend the Youth 2000 summer festival before flying to Medjugorje for the annual youth festival there, we'd stay there for twelve days. Then three or four of us would then travel to Rome for a few days, and then on to France for two weeks. We had a busy few weeks ahead of us, but we both looked forward to the adventure. Our journey was starting and would be ending in France.

We arrived in the south of France and spent a few hours by the sea in Biarritz. After which we travelled to Bayonne to meet with Francesca and Cristina. We then had a short train journey to St Jean Pied de Port. This was the official starting point of our journey. It is a small town at the foot of the Pyrenees mountain range. Upon arrival we went and registered for the pilgrimage. We received our pilgrim passport, which had to be stamped at every hostel we stayed in along the way. These passports needed to be shown in the pilgrim office in Santiago as proof of our pilgrimage. We were also given maps that showed distances between towns, with the gradients and a list of hostels known as 'albergues' along the way. We could plan our walking, knowing exactly how far we had to travel each day. After receiving everything, we went to our first hostel. It had been a long day and we were all hungry. After signing in, we left our bags on our beds and the four of us went out for a meal. Afterwards we strolled around looking at the small town before going to bed.

The following morning we got up early. After breakfast I bought four scallop shells from the hostel owner. The scallop shell is a symbol of Pilgrimage. Many meanings have been placed on this, one being that; in past times pilgrims used the shells to drink water from streams and rivers. After taking some photographs outside the hostel we began walking. Our first day was going to be a very tough introduction to the pilgrimage. We were walking up the Pyrenees and staying in a hostel near the top that night. It was a twenty-seven-kilometer walk and I found it extremely hard. We walked for hours in the mountains. The views were amazingly spectacular and stretched out for kilometers. While we walked, we chatted and prayed with one another. On occasions, we spent time alone taking in our surroundings. After several hours, I was walking alone and talking with God. I was conversing with him about my journey in life thus far. I was also listening to a Catholic singer on my ipod. During one of the hymns, he meditates on the very thing that I had been talking with God about. As I listened to his words, I began to cry tears of sheer joy. I thought 'here I am making my way up the Pyrenees, and less than six years ago, I could not walk up my stairs at home without gasping for air'. I reflected on how good God has been to me as I continued walking towards Santiago.

At about 5pm we reached the hostel in Roncesvalles 27 kilometers later. Roncesvalles was a very welcome sight as our rest place for the night. On arrival we got our pilgrim passport stamped and got our beds for the night. Each hostel along the way only costs a few euros, some where donation only. Our beds where in a large room with many bunk beds. After a long day in the heat, a shower never felt as good. Afterwards we washed our clothes and spent sometime in the evening sunshine relaxing, talking and writing in Francesca's journal. We got Holy Mass and a pilgrim blessing before we had dinner in a local restaurant, again for a few euros. After dinner we planned our journey for the following day and settled down for an early night. Surprisingly my body did not ache as much as I had feared. My left knee had troubled me for the last number of kilometers of the journey. The following morning my body was a little stiff, but I was ready to begin walking again.

The next eighteen days consisted of walking, talking, praying, eating and sleeping. In the simplicity of this way of life, many things are experienced. I was pushing my body way beyond any limits I could ever have imagined, going through my illness. I really experienced how Gods design of the body is truly awesome. All of the bodily senses were used daily and appreciated walking the Camino, We experienced Gods wonderful creation with our hearing, sight, smell, taste and touch.

On our journey towards Santiago we passed many towns and villages and stayed in places such as Pamplona, Burgos, Castrojeriz, Leon, Villadangos, Astorga, Villafranca, La Faba, Fonfria, Sarria, Portomarin, Ribadiso and Palas de Rei. Each place very different to each other. We arrived in a crowed Pamplona on the first day of the famous bull running festival. We had to sleep outside the train station, as there where no room in any of the hostels, an experience we will never forget. Each day brought its own challenge. Along the way we even got separated from Cristina a few times. She had walked ahead with a small group of mainly Italians pilgrims. We always caught up with her a few days later. Thus Rob, Francesca and myself spent a number of days traveling together, especially towards the end of the pilgrimage. However Cristina kept walking and arrived in Santiago two days ahead of us.

The last few days walking was a wonderful time. We spoke of our relationships with God and shared more of our own lives with one another. Spending so much time together intensified our relationships. A deeper friendship grew between Rob and myself, while a new friendship with Francesca began to blossom. We shared many wonderful experiences and have many memories to last us our lifetimes. I highly recommend the Camino de Santiago to everyone. Especially anyone who likes a physical challenge, or wants to discover God or maybe just wants to take time away to think things over. On the way one learns a lot about oneself and learns to appreciate everything one has and is given by God.

On the morning of July 24th we started walking at 7am. It was the last number of kilometers of our pilgrimage. We were getting excited as the destination was so close. Walking on this day seemed easier than any other. We arrived at the Cathedral in Santiago de Compestela at 12-noon, just in time for Holy Mass. During Mass I was overcome with emotion and I cried with joy. I thanked God for His goodness. The reality and enormity of what I had achieved began to sink in, we had walked 450 kilometers in nineteen days. The full french Camino is just under 800km, we took a train and a bus to skip a few hundred kilometers, we walked fully from Leon all the way to Santiago de Compestela. I was extremely happy. I thanked God for Rob, Francesca and Cristina whom we had reunited with in the Cathedral. After mass we went for lunch with some of our fellow pilgrims. Afterwards however, our walking was not finished. The three of us had to find accommodation, so we said goodbye to Cristina who had decided her journey was not over. She was walking for a further three days to Finisterre on the coast. All the hostels in Santiago were full and we eventually found a small hotel outside Santiago which we booked into for two nights. After showering and resting we went back into town that evening and had a great night of celebration.

My words are too poor to convey what the Camino has meant to me. I guess it's a special gift from God to able to walk the Camino. It's a very personal pilgrimage with God and your fellow pilgrims. The only way one can experience the Camino, is by making that first step and saying 'I will walk the Camino de Santiago'. That is when the pilgrimage truly begins.

I recently heard a talk by a Dominican priest friend of mine, Fr. John Harris OP, at a youth 2000 retreat. It made me think of my walk on the Camino de Santiago. He said that mankind has four basic needs, to eat, to drink, to belong and to be loved. He said only God can fulfill each of these needs. Thinking about the Camino, these basic needs were very important and forefront in our minds. Each evening we planned for the following day. Where would we eat? Do we need to buy food? Where would we sleep? We always had to make sure that we had enough water to drink, as somedays were extremely hot. We really felt 'belonged' and 'loved' in our small little group. Traveling to Santiago as a group made it easier. In the simplicity of daily living we supported and took care of each other. We met incredible people along the way, from locals, hostel owners and our fellow pilgrims. They all showed us a generous love that surpassed any of the language barriers that Myself and Rob encountered. We both thanked God on many occasions for Francesca, who could speak several languages. Grazie Mille Fra.

As I listened to Fr. John, I had the Realisation that God was truly present each step of the way. Even if I didn't see it at the time. He was with us daily at Holy Mass. His wonderful creation was our Way, even every steep hill that I greeted with a sigh and moan. Once again Rob and Francesca, I'm sorry for testing your patients to the limit. God was very present in each of us, to one another and the people we met. After Fr. John's talk, I began comparing the Camino with my journey to God in Heaven. Each day towards Heaven should be planned, just as on the Camino. To live well we must go to God for our basic needs. In doing so, we know that we are Loved, we have a sense of belonging to the communion of Saints, and we are nourished with Jesus in the Eucharist. Jesus gave us His precious body and blood in the most basic of food and drink, bread and wine. He knew how accessible they are for all of mankind. I must admit, that I take receiving Holy Communion for granted many times. I need to improve my understanding and reverence of this most Holy Sacrament and come to receive the Body and Blood of Christ with a Pure Heart. I pray that God gives me the Grace to have a pure heart, only in this way will I get to see God. Our goal in life, is to get to Heaven. Something that occurred to me as I reflected on this was, the joy in my heart as I saw the road sign for Santiago. The journey was nearly complete, but we had to keep going until we reached our destination. Just like our journey to God, its not over till we're in Heaven. The Camino de Santiago is a journey I will never forget and I thank God for the opportunity of walking along the Way with Rob, Francesca and Cristina.

Our trips to Medjugorje and Rome where fantastic and a great blessing. About Sixty of us connected to Pure In Heart, members and family enjoyed the youth festival in Medjugorje. After twelve days in Medjugorje Rob, Kevin and Myself got a ferry from Split, Croatia to Ancona, Italy. We travelled on to Rome by train. It was my first time to visit Rome and we got to see Pope Benedict XVI and pray at Pope John Paul II's tomb while there. It was a superb way to finish of our summer of pilgrimages.

As for France, Myself and Rob never made it for our two week pilgrimage. A couple of days into the Camino, we both felt the Holy Spirit telling us not to go ahead with that planned portion of our Pilgrimage. We had both worried about telling the other that we wanted to cancel. I said it to Rob one morning and to my surprise he was relieved. He was feeling the same. Then a couple of days later we got an email from Catriona in Ireland saying that she would not be able to travel to France as planned. We then had to inform Kevin of our decision, thankfully he was ok about having to cancel going to France.

They say in your life, you meet people for a reason, a season or for a lifetime. I know that I've learnt so much from the many wonderful people that I've met and I continue to meet. These people have shaped my life and helped me on my journey. I pray that I meet many more wonderful people who will inspire me. Such people have already made me praise and thank God for each new day of life that I've been gifted.

My book is coming to an end now. For me writing it has been a joy, a blessing and a challenge. God has amazed me with His goodness for each new chapter that has come since my transplant. My life gets better with each new day. It's January 2008 as I put the finishing touches to this book, but thank God my story is not finished just yet.

By reading my story I hope it inspires you. I still find it amazing that God could melt my hard heart. In that beautiful moment at the Blue Cross in Medjugorje, He poured all His love into my Heart. I pray that you come to know Him in an even more Beautiful and Special way. Discovering Him in a way that you never knew, or ever imagined could exist. Knowing and feeling Gods Love is the greatest joy on earth. Remember, God is Love and He loves you just as you are.

May God the Father, Son and Holy Spirit always bless and protect you in your moments of God. Our Blessed Mother Mary brought me back to her Son, Jesus. I thank Her for that moment of intercession with Her Son. As my journey continues, I will keep you in my prayers,

God bless and please keep me in your prayers. Remember that God is good, all the time...

Buen Camino.
Ken

P.S. St. Raphael, the journey still amazes me!!!!

Dedication:
I would like to dedicate this book to my Nana Vera, and the memory of my deceased grandparents, Thomas, Frank and Kathleen. Also for all my deceased Cystic Fibrosis friends and especially for my Donor and his family for the gift of life. Rest in Peace.

Acknowledgements:
I'd especially like to thank my family, parents Anne and David, my sister Lorna and my brother Gary for all their love and support throughout my life. To all my family and friends for always being there for me too. I want to thank Cyrelle my now brother-in-law for supporting Lorna when things got rough for me. Thanks to Evelyn, my Sister in law too, she just missed out on all the madness. Thanks to all my neighbours and priests of the parish for their prayers and support. Thanks to everyone who prayed for me, especially those of you around the world, who have never met me. God will bless your kindness.

Thanks to all the priests, friends and visionaries in Medjugorje for your prayers, and for your witness for God since that faithful day in June 1981. 'Hvala ti' to

Kris in Colombo Restaurant who has been a good friend of mine since 1998 and has looked after me every time I've returned to Medjugorje, I can never repay all you've done for me.

Thanks to all the doctors, nurses, surgeons and everyone connected with all the hospitals I've ever attended.

Special thanks to the Henry, Collins and Pykett families for your friendship, you're all just like family. Thanks to baby Christina and Jack Murphy for cheering me up when I was practically living in hospital in 2001, they are no longer babies may I add. A very special thank you to my donor and his family for the precious gift of life. Thanks to everyone in Pure In Heart and Youth 2000 for your prayerful support and treasured friendships. Thanks to all the wonderful Priests I am blessed to know and call friends, I pray God continues to inspire your vocation.

Big Thanks to all who have helped in reading the many draft copies of my book. Your words of encouragement and wisdom are appreciated. Thank you Ross for your editing and advice, I know it is a long time ago since you did all the hard work. Thank you Lorna for your design expertise and advise.

A HUGE thank you to my 2 Beautiful nephews, James and Luka who were both born after I finished writing this book and are now my new best friends. They've brought great Joy and Love to me, their Parents, Grandparents and all the family.

Finally, Thanks to Our Blessed Mother Mary, for leading me back to her Son Jesus. Praise and Thanksgiving to God the Father, the Son, and Holy Spirit now and forever, Amen

Website:
I've put together a website. It's a follow up to my book with story updates and photos of the many places I've travelled. Plus much more for you to explore..!!!

Here is the Web address:
http://kenparkes113.wix.com/moments

To order copies of my book, go to following Link:
http://www.lulu.com/spotlight/kenparkes111